NORMANDY

TRAVEL GUIDE

2024 EDITION

TABLE OF CONTENTS

NOTE:

Embark upon an unparalleled journey as you immerse yourself in the very essence of this Normandy travel guide. Crafted not only to inform but to spark your imagination, nurture your creativity, and awaken the adventurer within you, this guide extends an invitation to step into a realm of exploration that is distinctly your own. Departing from the ordinary, you won't find accompanying images within these pages. Our firm belief rests in the idea that the true beauty of every discovery is most vividly experienced firsthand, untainted by visual interpretations or preconceived notions.

Picture every monument, each destination, and even the hidden corners of Normandy as exquisite surprises, patiently awaiting the moment to captivate and astonish you when you find yourself standing before them. We are steadfast in our commitment to preserving the thrill of that initial gaze, the sheer wonder that accompanies the revelation of something new. With this guide in hand, you stand on the precipice of an extraordinary voyage where curiosity is your sole mode of transportation, and this guide serves as your unwavering companion. Set aside any preconceived notions and allow yourself to be transported into an authentic Normandy of revelations—the enchantment of your adventure begins right here. However, keep in mind that the most enchanting images will be the ones etched by your own eyes and treasured within your heart.

In stark contrast to conventional guidebooks, this volume intentionally omits intricate maps. The reason, you may ask? We ardently believe that the most extraordinary discoveries unfurl when you let yourself lose track, allowing the very essence of each place to guide you while embracing the uncertainty of the path. Bid farewell to predetermined itineraries and meticulously laid out routes, for our aim is to empower you to navigate Normandy in your very own way, unburdened by boundaries. Allow yourself to be carried by the currents of exploration, uncovering hidden gems that remain elusive on conventional maps. Summon the courage to embrace the unknown, trusting your instincts as you boldly venture forth, prepared to be pleasantly surprised—because the magic of your journey starts now, in a realm where maps are nonexistent, and the paths unfold with each step. The most extraordinary adventures await within the uncharted folds of the unfamiliar.

INTRODUCTION

Welcome to Normandy

Welcome to Normandy, a region that encapsulates the quintessential beauty of France, offering a rich tapestry of history, culture, and natural wonders. As you step into this picturesque land, you are greeted by rolling hills, lush landscapes, and a coastline that stretches along the English Channel. This is a place where time seems to slow down, allowing you to immerse yourself in the charm of medieval towns, the solemnity of historic sites, and the warmth of local hospitality.

Normandy is a region that has etched its mark on the pages of history, playing a pivotal role in shaping the destiny of Europe. Its soil witnessed the infamous Battle of Normandy during World War II, and remnants of this tumultuous past can be explored on the solemn beaches of Omaha, Utah, Juno, Gold, and Sword. The echoes of history resound through the corridors of medieval castles, such as the majestic Château de Falaise, where William the Conqueror was born.

One cannot speak of Normandy without mentioning the iconic Mont Saint-Michel, a marvel of medieval architecture that stands proudly amidst the bay, defying the ebb and flow of the tides. This abbey, perched on a rocky island, is a testament to human ingenuity and the enduring spirit of the Normans. The ethereal beauty of Mont Saint-Michel has made it a UNESCO World Heritage site, attracting millions of visitors who seek to witness the magic of this architectural masterpiece.

As you traverse the winding roads of Normandy, you'll encounter charming villages that seem frozen in time. The half-timbered houses of Honfleur, with their vibrant colors and cobbled streets, exude a maritime charm that has inspired artists for centuries. The town's picturesque harbor, immortalized by painters like Claude Monet, invites you to savor the simple pleasures of life – a leisurely stroll along the quays, a freshly caught seafood meal, and the gentle lapping of waves against the boats.

Normandy's culinary scene is a feast for the senses, where gastronomy is an art form. Indulge in the region's famous Camembert and Brie cheeses, paired with a crisp baguette and a glass of local cider. The apple orchards of Normandy produce some of the finest cider and Calvados, offering a delightful tasting experience that reflects the region's agricultural abundance.

In the heart of Normandy, the city of Rouen stands as a testament to Gothic grandeur. The towering spires of Rouen Cathedral, immortalized by Claude Monet's series of paintings, dominate the city's skyline. Wander through the medieval streets of the Old Town, where timber-framed houses lean into each other, creating a charming maze that reveals surprises at every turn.

Normandy's beaches, with their golden sands and invigorating sea air, offer a haven for relaxation and recreation. Whether you choose to bask in the sun, take a refreshing dip in the Channel, or engage in water sports, the coastline beckons with its natural beauty and serenity. The Normandy coastline is a playground for nature enthusiasts, with hidden cliffs, dramatic rock formations, and picturesque coastal trails waiting to be explored.

As the sun sets over Normandy, casting a warm glow over the landscape, you'll find that the region's beauty extends beyond its physical allure. It lies in the welcoming smiles of the locals, the genuine conversations in charming cafés, and the sense of community that permeates every corner. Normandy invites you not just to be a spectator but to be an active participant in its story – a story of resilience, cultural richness, and a deep connection to the land.

In conclusion, welcome to Normandy, where every cobblestone has a story to tell, every castle whispers of a bygone era, and every landscape invites you to become a part of its timeless tale. Whether you seek the thrill of history, the tranquility of nature, or the indulgence of culinary delights, Normandy welcomes you with open arms, promising an unforgettable journey through one of France's most enchanting regions.

About This Guide

Welcome to the Normandy Travel Guide, 2024 Edition! In the pages that follow, we embark on a journey through the picturesque landscapes, rich history, and vibrant culture of one of France's most enchanting regions. Whether you're a first-time visitor or a seasoned traveler returning to explore more, this guide is crafted to be your companion, offering insights, recommendations, and practical information to enhance your Normandy experience.

Normandy, situated in the northwestern part of France, is renowned for its captivating blend of coastal beauty, charming countryside, and historical significance. As you leaf through these pages, envision yourself strolling along the shores of the English Channel, wandering through quaint villages with half-timbered houses, and immersing yourself in the echoes of momentous events that have shaped this region.

This guide is designed to be a comprehensive resource, covering a myriad of aspects that make Normandy a must-visit destination. From practical travel tips to in-depth explorations of historical landmarks, culinary adventures, and outdoor activities, we strive to provide a holistic view of what this region has to offer.

Normandy is a diverse tapestry of experiences, and our recommendations aim to cater to a broad spectrum of interests. Whether you're a history buff intrigued by the D-Day Landing Beaches, a nature enthusiast seeking hiking trails, or a food lover eager to savor local delicacies, we've curated suggestions to ensure there's something for everyone.

As you delve into the guide, you'll find a seamless flow of information organized to assist you in planning your journey. While there are no strict subheadings in this section, the subsequent chapters are thoughtfully structured to guide you through various aspects of your trip, offering a balance between practical details and inspirational content.

Beyond the conventional tourist trail, we aim to provide you with glimpses of authentic Normandy—intimate cafes tucked away in cobblestone alleys, lesser-known historical gems, and opportunities to engage with the warm and welcoming locals. Let this guide be your key to unlocking the hidden treasures that make Normandy a unique and unforgettable destination.

This guide is not merely a compilation of facts; it's a dialogue with the reader. Feel free to engage with the content, adapt recommendations to suit your preferences, and use this guide as a flexible tool for crafting your personalized Normandy adventure. Whether you're seeking solitude on a quiet beach or the buzz of a local market, we encourage you to make this guide your own.

We understand that every traveler's experience is unique. If you discover a charming café not mentioned here or stumble upon a hidden gem, we invite you to share your insights. Your feedback is invaluable, contributing to the evolving tapestry of recommendations for future explorers.

Normandy awaits with open arms, ready to enchant you with its beauty and captivate you with its stories. As you embark on this adventure, may this guide be a trusted companion, offering not just information, but an invitation to immerse yourself fully in the magic that is Normandy. Bon voyage!

Quick Tips for Travelers

Normandy, with its rich history, picturesque landscapes, and vibrant culture, is a captivating destination for travelers. Whether you're a history buff exploring the D-Day landing beaches or a food enthusiast indulging in local delicacies, here are essential tips to ensure a seamless and memorable journey through this enchanting region.

Weather and Seasons:

Normandy experiences a temperate maritime climate. Summers are mild, making it an ideal time for outdoor activities, while winters are relatively cool. Pack accordingly, and be prepared for occasional rain showers.

Currency and Payments:

The official currency is the Euro. Credit cards are widely accepted in urban areas, but it's advisable to carry some cash, especially when exploring rural or less touristy areas.

Language:

French is the primary language spoken in Normandy. While many locals may understand basic English, learning a few common French phrases can enhance your experience and interactions.

Transportation:

Normandy is well-connected by trains, buses, and roads. Consider renting a car to explore remote areas. Public transportation is efficient for city-to-city travel, but a car provides flexibility for off-the-beaten-path adventures.

Cultural Etiquette:

Politeness is highly valued in French culture. Greet locals with a "Bonjour" and say "Merci" when receiving assistance. Tipping is customary, typically around 10% in restaurants.

Dining Experience:

Normandy is renowned for its gastronomy. Enjoy local specialties such as Camembert cheese, cider, and seafood. Don't rush meals; dining is a leisurely affair, so savor the flavors and embrace the relaxed pace.

Historical Sites and Museums:

Normandy is steeped in history, especially related to World War II. Plan visits to iconic sites like Mont Saint-Michel and the D-Day landing beaches. Consider guided tours to gain deeper insights into the region's historical significance.

Attire:

Casual wear is generally acceptable, but it's wise to bring layers, as weather conditions can vary. If you plan to visit religious sites or upscale restaurants, consider packing slightly more formal attire.

Safety Precautions:

Normandy is a safe destination, but like any travel, exercise standard safety precautions. Keep an eye on your belongings in crowded areas and be cautious of your surroundings, particularly in urban centers.

Festivals and Events:

Check the local events calendar for festivals and cultural events taking place during your visit. Participating in festivities provides a unique opportunity to immerse yourself in Normandy's vibrant traditions.

Local Markets:

Explore the bustling markets, where you can find fresh produce, artisanal crafts, and local treats. Engage with vendors, sample regional products, and take home a piece of Normandy.

Nature and Outdoor Activities:

Normandy's diverse landscapes invite outdoor enthusiasts. Whether it's hiking along coastal cliffs or cycling through picturesque villages, embrace the natural beauty and serenity the region offers.

Accommodations:

Book accommodations in advance, especially during peak tourist seasons. Normandy offers a range of options, from charming bed and breakfasts to luxurious hotels. Choose accommodations that align with your travel style and preferences.

Connect with Locals:

Engage with locals to enhance your cultural experience. Attend community events, strike up conversations in cafés, and embrace the warmth of Normandy's hospitality.

Photography:

Capture the beauty of Normandy but be mindful of privacy. Ask for permission before photographing locals, and be aware of any restrictions in museums and historical sites.

Incorporating these tips into your travel plans will ensure a fulfilling and enjoyable journey through Normandy, leaving you with lasting memories of this enchanting region.

CHAPTER 1: DISCOVERING NORMANDY'S REGIONS

1. Upper Normandy

Upper Normandy, renowned for its picturesque landscapes and historic sites, is a captivating region waiting to be explored.

Rouen

Address: 3 Rue Jacques Villon, 76000 Rouen, France

Begin your journey in Rouen, the capital of Upper Normandy. Marvel at the stunning architecture of Rouen Cathedral and visit the Gros-Horloge, a medieval clock tower.

Giverny

Address: 84 Rue Claude Monet, 27620 Giverny, France

Art enthusiasts should not miss Giverny, home to Claude Monet's enchanting garden and house. The water lilies and vibrant flowers provide a living canvas straight out of Monet's paintings.

2. Lower Normandy

Lower Normandy, with its charming countryside and seaside vistas, offers a more relaxed pace of life.

Caen

Address: Esplanade General Eisenhower, 14050 Caen, France

Caen, a city with a rich history, is home to the Caen Memorial, dedicated to the events of World War II. Explore the medieval Château de Caen and stroll through the historic Vaugueux Quarter.

Bayeux

Address: 13 Rue de Nesmond, 14400 Bayeux, France

Visit Bayeux to witness the world-famous Bayeux Tapestry, a remarkable piece of medieval art depicting the Norman Conquest of England. The charming town also boasts the stunning Bayeux Cathedral.

3. The Cotentin Peninsula

The Cotentin Peninsula, surrounded by rugged coastline, offers a mix of history and natural beauty.

Cherbourg

Address: Quai de la France, 50100 Cherbourg-en-Cotentin, France

Cherbourg, a port city, houses the Cité de la Mer, an impressive maritime museum. Explore the historic Fort du Roule for panoramic views of the city and harbor.

Barfleur

Address: Rue Saint-Nicolas, 50760 Barfleur, France

For a taste of authentic Norman charm, visit Barfleur, a picturesque fishing village known for its cobbled streets and medieval architecture.

4. Pays d'Auge

Pays d'Auge, an idyllic countryside region, is famous for its apple orchards and traditional half-timbered houses.

Lisieux

Address: Basilique Sainte-Thérèse, 17 Rue Sainte-Thérèse, 14100 Lisieux, France

Lisieux is a pilgrimage site with the impressive Basilique Sainte-Thérèse. The town beautifully blends spirituality with Norman architecture.

5. Calvados

Calvados, named after the famous apple brandy, is a region known for its charming villages and coastal delights.

Honfleur

Address: Quai Sainte-Catherine, 14600 Honfleur, France

Honfleur, with its colorful harbor and narrow streets, is a haven for artists. Visit the Sainte-Catherine Church and explore the art galleries that line the Vieux Bassin.

Deauville

Address: 1 Avenue Lucien Barrière, 14800 Deauville, France

Deauville, a glamorous seaside resort, beckons with its casino, luxury hotels, and the famous Planches boardwalk.

1. Upper Normandy

Upper Normandy is a region of captivating beauty and historical significance, located in the northern part of France. Its diverse landscapes, rich cultural heritage, and charming towns make it a compelling destination for travelers seeking a blend of history, nature, and authentic French experiences.

Stretching along the English Channel, Upper Normandy encompasses a tapestry of landscapes that range from picturesque coastal areas to lush countryside. The Seine River, which meanders through the region, adds a touch of serenity to the scenery. One of the most iconic landmarks of

Upper Normandy is the stunning cliffs of Étretat, whose dramatic white chalk formations rise majestically from the azure waters below.

Rouen, the capital of Upper Normandy, stands as a testament to the region's historical significance. With its well-preserved medieval architecture, including the impressive Rouen Cathedral and the Gros Horloge clock, the city exudes an old-world charm. The cobblestone streets of the Old Town invite visitors to wander and discover the stories embedded in the city's past.

Upper Normandy is also known for its connection to the renowned artist Claude Monet. Giverny, a small village in the region, is where Monet lived and created some of his most famous works, including the Water Lilies series. The enchanting gardens at Monet's house are a haven for art enthusiasts and nature lovers alike, offering a glimpse into the inspiration behind the masterpieces.

In addition to its cultural treasures, Upper Normandy boasts a vibrant culinary scene. The region is celebrated for its dairy products, particularly its creamy cheeses such as Camembert and Neufchâtel. Visitors can indulge in the local gastronomy by exploring traditional markets, where farmers proudly showcase their fresh produce and artisanal creations.

For those seeking outdoor adventures, Upper Normandy doesn't disappoint. The Seine Maritime region offers opportunities for hiking and cycling, allowing travelers to explore the scenic countryside at their own pace. The Alabaster Coast, with its high cliffs and pebble beaches, provides a picturesque backdrop for leisurely strolls and contemplative moments.

The historic significance of Upper Normandy is deeply intertwined with the events of World War II. The Normandy American Cemetery and Memorial in Colleville-sur-Mer stands as a poignant tribute to the Allied forces who sacrificed their lives during the D-Day landings. Visiting this solemn site is a moving experience that underscores the region's role in shaping world history.

Upper Normandy's smaller towns and villages contribute to the region's unique character. Honfleur, with its charming harbor and timber-framed houses, is a delightful destination that has inspired artists for centuries. Le Havre, a UNESCO World Heritage site, showcases modernist architecture amid its historical roots, offering a fascinating blend of past and present.

In conclusion, Upper Normandy beckons travelers with its blend of natural beauty, historical landmarks, and cultural richness. Whether exploring the medieval streets of Rouen, marveling at the coastal cliffs of Étretat, or immersing oneself in the artistic legacy of Claude Monet, this region invites visitors to embark on a journey of discovery and appreciation for the timeless allure of Upper Normandy.

Rouen

Rouen, the capital of the Upper Normandy region in northwestern France, stands as a testament to the rich history and cultural heritage that characterizes this enchanting city. As one of the best-preserved medieval cities in Europe, Rouen beckons visitors with its stunning architecture, historic landmarks, and vibrant atmosphere.

The city's crowning jewel is undoubtedly the Rouen Cathedral, a masterpiece of French Gothic architecture. Its soaring spires and intricate façade draw the eyes of both pilgrims and art enthusiasts alike. The cathedral's construction spanned several centuries, resulting in a harmonious blend of architectural styles that tell the story of Rouen's enduring history.

Adjacent to the cathedral is the Gros-Horloge, a mesmerizing astronomical clock that has been keeping time since the 14th century. The ornate clock face, adorned with zodiac signs and mythical figures, is a captivating sight. Visitors can climb to the top of the belfry for panoramic views of Rouen's charming streets and the Seine River.

Rouen's medieval charm extends to its old town, a labyrinth of narrow cobbled streets, half-timbered houses, and hidden squares. Stroll through the Vieux Marché, where Joan of Arc, the iconic French heroine, met her tragic end. The Place du Vieux Marché remains a central hub, surrounded by cafes and shops, offering a glimpse into daily life in this historic city.

Art enthusiasts will find solace in the Musée des Beaux-Arts de Rouen, an art museum that houses an impressive collection spanning from the Middle Ages to the 20th century. The museum showcases works by renowned artists such as Monet, Delacroix, and Caravaggio, providing a visual journey through the evolution of art.

For those seeking a deeper connection to Rouen's past, a visit to the Aître Saint-Maclou is a must. This historical site, once a mass grave for plague victims, is now a tranquil courtyard surrounded by intricately carved wooden buildings. The macabre yet fascinating atmosphere offers a glimpse into the challenges faced by Rouen throughout the centuries.

Rouen's allure extends beyond its medieval core. The city embraces modernity with the strikingly contemporary Church of Saint Joan of Arc, a tribute to the city's most famous historical figure. The church's unique design incorporates both traditional and modern elements, creating a symbolic and architectural landmark.

Culinary delights await in Rouen's restaurants and bistros, where local specialties take center stage. Indulge in Normandy's famous Camembert cheese, sip on a glass of the region's

renowned apple cider, and savor a hearty meal featuring fresh seafood sourced from the nearby coast.

As the day winds down, the Quais de Seine beckon. This scenic area along the riverbank offers a perfect setting for a leisurely evening stroll. The illuminated buildings cast a warm glow over the water, creating a magical ambiance that encapsulates the timeless beauty of Rouen.

In conclusion, Rouen stands as a living canvas, where every cobblestone and building tells a story. The city's ability to seamlessly blend its medieval past with a vibrant present makes it a destination that caters to a diverse range of interests. Whether you're a history buff, art lover, or simply in search of an authentic French experience, Rouen welcomes you with open arms, inviting you to uncover the layers of its rich tapestry.

Giverny: A Tapestry of Nature and Art

Nestled in the heart of the French countryside, Giverny stands as a testament to the intersection of nature and art. This quaint village, located in the Upper Normandy region, is perhaps best known as the residence of the renowned Impressionist painter Claude Monet. Giverny's allure extends beyond the canvas, inviting visitors to immerse themselves in the vibrant landscapes that once inspired one of the art world's most celebrated masters.

The undulating hills and meandering Seine River provide a breathtaking backdrop to Giverny's natural beauty. Spring ushers in a riot of colors as the famous gardens burst into bloom. Wisteria-draped bridges span over ponds filled with water lilies, reflecting the changing hues of the surrounding flora. Monet's deliberate arrangement of flowers and plants transforms Giverny into a living masterpiece, a canvas that evolves with the seasons.

Strolling through the Clos Normand, Monet's flower garden, is like navigating a kaleidoscope of colors. Delicate irises, fragrant roses, and cheerful sunflowers create a sensory feast. The Japanese bridge, immortalized in Monet's paintings, arches gracefully over the water, leading visitors into a dreamscape of weeping willows and water lilies.

Beyond the Clos Normand lies the Water Garden, a tranquil oasis that served as the muse for Monet's iconic Water Lilies series. The lily pads, seemingly suspended on the water's surface, cast reflections that dance with the rhythm of nature. Giverny's gardens are a testament to Monet's passion for horticulture and his keen ability to capture the ephemeral beauty of the natural world.

At the heart of Giverny stands Monet's residence, a charming pink farmhouse where the artist lived for over four decades. The house, with its green shutters and flower-covered façade, exudes a warm invitation. Stepping inside is like entering Monet's private realm, where every room tells a story of his life and creative process.

Monet's studio, bathed in soft northern light, remains much as it was during his time. Easels and paintbrushes stand frozen in a perpetual state of creation. The dining room, adorned with Japanese prints that influenced Monet's work, echoes with the laughter of the artist's large family and friends who gathered here.

The vibrant yellow dining room, overlooking the Clos Normand, served as a gathering place for Monet and his guests. The sunlit space, adorned with blue tiles and a collection of Japanese prints, encapsulates the convivial spirit that permeated Monet's home.

While Monet's legacy is indelibly woven into the fabric of Giverny, the village has embraced a broader artistic identity. The American Impressionist Art Museum, located just steps away from Monet's residence, showcases a diverse collection of Impressionist paintings. The museum provides a context for Monet's work, placing it within the broader narrative of the Impressionist movement.

Giverny also serves as a haven for contemporary artists. The Giverny Impressionism Festival, an annual event, celebrates the village's artistic heritage through exhibitions, workshops, and performances. Local galleries showcase a diverse range of works, from traditional landscapes to avant-garde installations.

For those seeking to immerse themselves in the beauty of Giverny, practical considerations are essential. The village is easily accessible from Paris, with a train journey to Vernon followed by a short bus ride to Giverny. The gardens are open to the public from spring to autumn, allowing visitors to witness the ever-changing tableau of colors.

Giverny's charm extends to its local cuisine. Visitors can savor the flavors of Normandy in the village's quaint eateries, offering dishes inspired by the region's fresh produce and culinary traditions.

In conclusion, Giverny stands as a testament to the symbiotic relationship between art and nature. Monet's gardens are not merely a tourist attraction; they are a living canvas that continues to inspire awe and admiration. Giverny's allure lies not only in its artistic legacy but in its ability to transport visitors to a realm where the boundary between the artist's vision and the natural world dissolves. As the seasons change, Giverny remains a timeless testament to the beauty that unfolds when nature and art harmonize in perfect unity.

2. Lower Normandy

Lower Normandy, a picturesque region in northwestern France, captivates visitors with its enchanting landscapes, rich history, and cultural treasures. Stretching from the windswept shores of the English Channel to the lush inland countryside, Lower Normandy beckons travelers to explore its diverse offerings.

The coastline of Lower Normandy is a tapestry of rugged cliffs, sandy beaches, and quaint fishing villages. One of the jewels of the region is the charming port town of Honfleur. Nestled at the mouth of the Seine River, Honfleur's narrow cobblestone streets and colorful timber-framed houses create a postcard-perfect scene. Visitors can stroll along the Vieux Bassin, the old harbor, lined with seafood restaurants and art galleries, capturing the essence of maritime life.

Moving westward along the coast, the D-Day Landing Beaches stand as solemn reminders of the pivotal events of World War II. Omaha Beach, Utah Beach, and Juno Beach, among others, bear witness to the courage and sacrifice of Allied forces. The Normandy American Cemetery, overlooking Omaha Beach, provides a poignant memorial to those who gave their lives for freedom.

Inland, the landscape transforms into rolling hills, verdant meadows, and charming villages. The historic town of Bayeux, with its well-preserved medieval architecture, is renowned for the Bayeux Tapestry—a remarkable embroidered cloth depicting the Norman Conquest of England in 1066. This UNESCO-listed treasure draws history enthusiasts from around the globe.

Nature enthusiasts find solace in Lower Normandy's lush countryside, where apple orchards and dairy farms dot the landscape. The Pays d'Auge region is famous for its pastoral beauty and traditional half-timbered houses. Visitors can savor the flavors of the region, including the world-famous Camembert cheese and Calvados, an apple brandy deeply rooted in Normandy's heritage.

Lower Normandy also offers a wealth of outdoor activities. Hiking trails crisscross the landscape, leading adventurers through forests, along riverbanks, and up to panoramic viewpoints. The Cotentin Peninsula, surrounded by the sea on three sides, invites exploration of its wild cliffs and serene coastal paths.

For those seeking architectural marvels, Lower Normandy boasts impressive châteaux and abbeys. The Abbey of Mont Saint-Michel, a UNESCO World Heritage site, rises dramatically from the sea on a rocky islet. Its stunning medieval architecture and intricate abbey church make it one of France's most iconic landmarks.

As evening falls, Lower Normandy's towns come alive with a vibrant culinary scene. Seafood takes center stage, with fresh catches from the English Channel gracing the menus of seaside eateries. Cozy bistros in the countryside serve up hearty Norman dishes, often accompanied by the region's renowned ciders and apple-based liqueurs.

Accommodations in Lower Normandy cater to a range of tastes and budgets. Charming bed and breakfasts offer personalized experiences, while historic manor houses and modern hotels provide comfort and luxury. Camping enthusiasts can find idyllic sites nestled in the countryside, allowing for a closer connection to nature.

In conclusion, Lower Normandy is a region that effortlessly blends history, nature, and gastronomy. Its diverse landscapes, from the windswept coastline to the serene countryside, offer a myriad of experiences for every traveler. Whether exploring historic sites, indulging in local delicacies, or simply soaking in the natural beauty, Lower Normandy promises an unforgettable journey through the heart of French heritage.

Caen

Caen, a city steeped in history and culture, stands as a testament to the resilience and renewal of the human spirit. Nestled in the heart of Lower Normandy, France, Caen has witnessed centuries of triumphs and tribulations, leaving an indelible mark on its landscape and character.

Caen's roots can be traced back to the Roman era, and its evolution is a compelling narrative of conquests, wars, and reconstruction. One of the city's most notable landmarks, the Château de Caen, is a formidable fortress that has stood witness to the ebb and flow of history. Built by William the Conqueror in the 11th century, the castle served as a strategic stronghold and a symbol of Norman power.

The city's medieval charm Is further exemplified by the Abbaye-aux-Hommes and the Abbaye-aux-Dames, two magnificent abbeys founded by William the Conqueror and his wife Matilda. These structures, with their soaring arches and intricate stone carvings, stand as architectural marvels that transport visitors to a bygone era.

Caen's significance extends beyond its medieval heritage; it holds a poignant connection to one of the darkest chapters of the 20th century—the Second World War. The Caen Memorial, erected in 1988, stands as a solemn tribute to the victims of war and a testament to the city's post-war reconstruction.

The memorial complex includes the Peace Museum, which provides a comprehensive overview of the events leading up to and during World War II. Through immersive exhibits, visitors gain insights into the impact of conflict on individuals and societies. The Memorial also features beautifully landscaped gardens and the Garden of Canada, a touching homage to the Canadian soldiers who played a pivotal role in the liberation of Normandy.

Caen is not merely a city frozen in time; it is a vibrant urban center that seamlessly blends its rich history with modernity. The city's streets are lined with bustling markets, charming cafés, and boutiques, offering a delightful mix of the traditional and the contemporary.

The Place Saint-Sauveur, a picturesque square surrounded by half-timbered houses, is a hub of activity. Here, locals and visitors alike gather to savor the flavors of Normandy in the welcoming ambiance of cafés and restaurants. The rhythm of daily life in Caen is underscored by the eclectic mix of street performers, artists, and vendors who bring the city's public spaces to life.

Caen's cultural vibrancy extends to its role as an educational center. The University of Caen Normandy, founded in 1432, is a venerable institution that has nurtured generations of scholars. The university's sprawling campus adds a youthful energy to the city, as students from across the globe converge to pursue knowledge in the shadow of historic landmarks.

No exploration of Caen would be complete without indulging in the culinary treasures that define Normandy's gastronomy. The city's markets brim with fresh produce, artisanal cheeses, and the famed apple-based products that the region is renowned for.

Visitors can savor the local delicacies in the charming bistros and eateries scattered throughout the city. From creamy Camembert to delectable seafood dishes, Caen's culinary scene is a celebration of the terroir that defines Normandy.

Caen's architectural landscape is a harmonious blend of Gothic masterpieces and modern structures. The Church of Saint-Pierre, with its soaring spires and intricate stained glass windows, is a testament to the city's religious heritage. In contrast, the contemporary Caen tramway gracefully winds its way through the city, connecting its diverse neighborhoods.

Caen's allure is not confined to its urban spaces; the city is surrounded by lush greenery and scenic landscapes. The Prairie district, with its expansive parks and gardens, provides a tranquil escape from the hustle and bustle of city life. The banks of the Orne River offer idyllic spots for leisurely strolls, inviting residents and visitors to connect with nature.

Throughout the year, Caen comes alive with a myriad of festivals and events that reflect its cultural dynamism. The Festival Beauregard, a music festival held in the grounds of the Château de Beauregard, attracts music enthusiasts from near and far. The Journées Médiévales, or Medieval Days, transport the city back in time, with reenactments, parades, and festivities that evoke the spirit of the Middle Ages.

In essence, Caen is more than a city—it is a living canvas that tells the story of Normandy and its people. From the echoes of medieval knights within the stone walls of the Château de Caen to the poignant reflections at the Caen Memorial, every corner of the city narrates a chapter of its storied past.

As Caen continues to evolve, embracing the future while honoring its heritage, it remains a destination that captivates the imagination and leaves an indelible mark on the hearts of those fortunate enough to explore its streets and savor its unique charm.

Bayeux

Bayeux, a town nestled in the heart of Normandy, France, holds a tapestry of history, culture, and charm that unfolds in every cobblestone street and medieval building. Its significance is anchored in the world-famous Bayeux Tapestry, an extraordinary piece of medieval art that draws visitors from across the globe. As one navigates the narrow lanes and squares, the town's rich heritage comes to life, narrating tales of conquests, resilience, and a timeless connection to the past.

The central jewel of Bayeux, both metaphorically and literally, is the Bayeux Tapestry. Housed in a specially designed museum, this masterpiece of embroidery stretches over 230 feet, recounting the story of the Norman Conquest of England in 1066. Stitched onto linen with exquisite craftsmanship, the tapestry takes viewers on a visual journey through history, capturing the epic Battle of Hastings and the events leading to William the Conqueror's triumph.

Beyond the renowned tapestry, Bayeux unfolds with a captivating blend of medieval and modern elements. The town's architectural tapestry includes the majestic Bayeux Cathedral, an awe-inspiring example of Gothic architecture. Dedicated to St. Andrew, this cathedral has stood witness to centuries of change and is a testament to the enduring spirit of Bayeux.

Wandering through the historic center, one encounters charming half-timbered houses, their beams weathered by time but standing strong. The Place de la Liberté, a bustling square surrounded by cafes and shops, serves as a focal point for locals and visitors alike. Here, the rhythm of daily life harmonizes with the echoes of history, creating a vibrant atmosphere that is uniquely Bayeux.

The tranquility of the River Aure, gently flowing through Bayeux, adds to the town's allure. Riverside walks offer peaceful moments, with glimpses of the cathedral's spires reflecting in the

water. Crossing the old stone bridges, one can sense the timeless connection between Bayeux and its natural surroundings.

Bayeux has not only preserved its medieval heritage but has also embraced modernity without sacrificing its essence. Quaint boutiques, offering a mix of local crafts and contemporary designs, line the streets. Cafes invite patrons to savor the flavors of Normandy, from buttery croissants to the renowned Camembert cheese.

For those seeking a deeper understanding of Bayeux's past, the Battle of Normandy Museum provides insight into the events leading up to and following D-Day during World War II. The museum's exhibits, artifacts, and immersive displays convey the courage and sacrifice of those who played a role in the Allied liberation of Normandy.

As evening descends, Bayeux transforms into a picturesque scene, with the cathedral and other landmarks illuminated against the night sky. The town's ambiance becomes more intimate, and the sounds of laughter and clinking glasses emanate from the local bistros.

Bayeux's hospitality extends beyond its architectural and historical marvels. Accommodations ranging from cozy bed and breakfasts to elegant hotels offer a comfortable haven for visitors. Many establishments exude a warm, familial charm, reflecting the genuine hospitality that is a hallmark of Normandy.

Venturing just beyond the town's borders reveals a landscape that further enriches the Bayeux experience. The Normandy countryside, with its rolling hills and orchards, beckons explorers. Day trips to nearby attractions, such as the D-Day Landing Beaches and the picturesque town of Arromanches-les-Bains, provide a broader context of the region's significance.

In every corner of Bayeux, there is a sense of continuity—a thread that weaves the present with the past. Whether standing before the Bayeux Tapestry, walking the ancient streets, or savoring the local cuisine, one is immersed in a living narrative that transcends time. Bayeux stands as a testament to the enduring legacy of Normandy, inviting all who visit to become a part of its remarkable tapestry.

3.   _The Cotentin Peninsula_

The Cotentin Peninsula, situated in the northwestern part of France, is a captivating region known for its rich history, diverse landscapes, and unique cultural heritage. This peninsula, often referred to as the "wild west" of Normandy, extends into the English Channel, creating a distinctive blend of coastal charm and rural beauty.

The rugged coastline of the Cotentin is a tapestry of dramatic cliffs, sandy beaches, and quaint fishing villages. One of the most iconic landmarks along this stretch is the Nez de Jobourg, boasting the highest cliffs in mainland Normandy. The sea has sculpted the shoreline into a series of picturesque bays and coves, offering visitors a serene escape from the hustle and bustle of urban life.

As you venture further inland, the landscape transforms into a patchwork of rolling hills, lush meadows, and charming farmlands. The Cotentin is renowned for its pastoral beauty, with traditional stone cottages nestled amidst fields of vibrant crops. The agricultural practices here have deep-rooted traditions, and the local markets showcase an abundance of fresh produce, dairy, and seafood.

History echoes through the Cotentin Peninsula, with evidence of its past visible in the form of medieval churches, historic manors, and remnants of World War II. The town of Cherbourg-Octeville, a major port on the northern coast, is a gateway to the peninsula's fascinating past. The Cité de la Mer, a maritime museum housed in an old transatlantic terminal, provides a captivating journey through maritime history, including exhibits on the Titanic.

One cannot explore the Cotentin without encountering the remnants of the D-Day landings in June 1944. Utah Beach, one of the key landing sites, stands as a solemn memorial to the bravery of those who fought for freedom. The Normandy American Cemetery, overlooking the sea, serves as a poignant reminder of the sacrifices made during that pivotal moment in history.

Nature enthusiasts will find solace in the diverse ecosystems of the Cotentin. The Parc Naturel Régional des Marais du Cotentin et du Bessin, a regional natural park, is a haven for birdwatchers and lovers of wetland habitats. The marshes and lagoons teem with birdlife, providing a serene backdrop for those seeking a tranquil escape into nature.

Cultural traditions thrive in the Cotentin Peninsula, with local festivals and events celebrating the region's unique identity. From lively fêtes in charming villages to traditional music and dance performances, visitors can immerse themselves in the authentic rhythms of Cotentin life.

The culinary scene of the Cotentin is a delightful exploration of regional flavors. Seafood, including the renowned Cotentin oysters, takes center stage in many local dishes. Traditional recipes passed down through generations showcase the abundance of fresh, locally sourced ingredients.

In conclusion, the Cotentin Peninsula is a treasure trove of natural beauty, historical significance, and cultural richness. Whether you seek the tranquility of coastal landscapes, the exploration of wartime history, or the charm of rural life, the Cotentin welcomes you with open arms. This hidden gem within Normandy invites travelers to uncover its secrets, each corner revealing a new facet of this enchanting ppeninsula

Cherbourg

Cherbourg, a historic port city nestled on the shores of the English Channel in Normandy, France, boasts a rich maritime heritage and a tapestry of cultural and architectural treasures. This coastal gem has witnessed centuries of history, from its strategic importance during medieval times to its role in significant naval events. In this exploration of Cherbourg, we delve into the city's past, present, and the myriad attractions that make it a captivating destination.

The origins of Cherbourg trace back to ancient times, with evidence of human habitation dating to the prehistoric era. Over the centuries, it evolved into a bustling harbor, gaining prominence during the Middle Ages. Its strategic location made it a sought-after prize during various conflicts, and the city frequently changed hands between English and French rule.

One of Cherbourg's most notable historical landmarks is the Fort du Roule, perched atop a hill overlooking the city and the harbor. Originally constructed in the 18th century, the fort has witnessed military actions during different periods, including the Napoleonic Wars and World

War II. Visitors can explore its well-preserved ramparts, gaining panoramic views of Cherbourg's coastline.

The maritime significance of Cherbourg Is epitomized by the colossal Cité de la Mer, a maritime museum housed in the former transatlantic ocean liner terminal. This colossal structure pays homage to the city's maritime heritage and the vital role Cherbourg played in oceanic exploration. The museum showcases an extensive collection of marine artifacts, including submarines, diving suits, and exhibits on the history of transatlantic travel.

Cherbourg's harbor, one of the largest artificial harbors in the world, is not only a testament to human engineering but also a picturesque setting for a leisurely stroll. The Quai de la France, lined with charming cafes and shops, provides a perfect vantage point to observe the bustling maritime activities and the comings and goings of fishing boats.

For those interested in religious architecture, Cherbourg offers the striking Basilique Sainte-Trinité. This neo-Gothic masterpiece, completed in the 19th century, stands as a testament to the city's enduring spiritual heritage. The basilica's intricate stained glass windows and towering spires make it a captivating structure, drawing both pilgrims and admirers of architectural beauty.

Cherbourg's city center is a harmonious blend of historic charm and modern amenities. The Place Napoléon, a central square, is surrounded by elegant buildings and cafes, creating a welcoming atmosphere for locals and visitors alike. Exploring the narrow streets radiating from

the square reveals hidden gems, including quaint boutiques, patisseries, and local markets offering a taste of Normandy's culinary delights.

In addition to its historical and architectural allure, Cherbourg is a gateway to the scenic wonders of the Cotentin Peninsula. The rugged coastline, with its cliffs and hidden coves, beckons nature enthusiasts and hikers. A drive along the coastal roads unveils breathtaking views of the English Channel, providing a sense of the natural beauty that has captivated artists and writers throughout the ages.

Cherbourg's culinary scene is a delightful exploration of Normandy's gastronomic treasures. Seafood, sourced fresh from the surrounding waters, takes center stage in local dishes. From the iconic Norman oysters to moules marinières (mussels in white wine sauce), the city's restaurants offer a delectable journey through maritime flavors.

As evening descends upon Cherbourg, the city's lights reflect on the tranquil waters of the harbor, creating a magical ambiance. The Quai Alexandre III, lined with restaurants and bars, becomes a lively hub for locals and tourists alike. Cherbourg's nightlife is a celebration of its maritime spirit, with establishments offering a diverse range of entertainment, from live music to waterfront dance floors.

In conclusion, Cherbourg is a city that unfolds its treasures to those willing to explore its streets and delve into its history. Whether you are fascinated by maritime adventures, enchanted by architectural marvels, or simply seeking the tranquility of coastal landscapes, Cherbourg invites you to immerse yourself in a journey through time and culture. Each cobblestone street, each historic site, and each encounter with the locals adds to the tapestry of experiences that make Cherbourg a truly unique destination in the heart of Normandy.

Barfleur

Barfleur, a quaint and picturesque fishing village nestled on the Normandy coast of France, stands as a testament to the region's rich history, maritime heritage, and timeless charm. With its cobbled streets, medieval architecture, and a serene ambiance, Barfleur offers a retreat from the hustle and bustle of modern life. This small commune, situated in the Manche department, is not only a visual delight but also a destination that transports visitors back in time.

At the heart of Barfleur is its historic harbor, which has been a focal point for centuries. The harbor, surrounded by well-preserved stone houses, exudes an old-world charm that captivates visitors from the moment they arrive. The rhythmic bobbing of fishing boats in the gentle tide creates a soothing melody, echoing the village's deep connection to the sea.

One of the notable landmarks in Barfleur is the Church of Saint-Nicolas. This medieval church, dating back to the 11th century, is a masterpiece of Norman architecture. Its slender spire reaches towards the sky, a prominent silhouette against the coastal backdrop. The church has weathered the passage of time, bearing witness to the village's maritime history and serving as a symbol of faith for the locals.

Wandering through Barfleur's narrow streets is like stepping into a storybook. The tightly packed houses, adorned with colorful flowers and ivy-covered facades, create a postcard-perfect setting. The absence of modern structures allows visitors to immerse themselves fully in the medieval atmosphere, where each building tells a tale of the village's evolution over the centuries.

Beyond its aesthetic appeal, Barfleur boasts a rich maritime heritage. The sea has been both a source of livelihood and a companion to the villagers throughout history. Fishermen set out at dawn, returning with the day's catch to the welcoming embrace of the harbor. The maritime museum in Barfleur provides insights into the village's seafaring traditions, displaying artifacts, models of historic ships, and narratives of maritime adventures.

For those seeking panoramic views of the village and its surroundings, a visit to Gatteville-le-Phare is a must. This neighboring commune is home to the Gatteville lighthouse, one of the tallest in Europe. Climbing to the top rewards visitors with breathtaking views of the coastline, including the charming village of Barfleur and its harbor.

Barfleur's allure extends to its culinary offerings, with local seafood taking center stage. Visitors can indulge in freshly caught fish, crab, and other seafood delicacies at the village's waterfront restaurants. The combination of sea air, maritime vistas, and delectable cuisine creates a sensory experience that lingers in the memory.

Throughout the year, Barfleur hosts various events that celebrate its cultural heritage and provide a glimpse into local traditions. From maritime festivals that honor the village's seafaring legacy to religious processions that highlight its spiritual roots, these events add a layer of authenticity to the visitor's experience.

Barfleur's significance is not limited to its past; it continues to be a haven for artists and writers seeking inspiration from its timeless beauty. The play of light on the stone facades, the vibrant hues of fishing boats, and the ever-changing moods of the sea offer endless inspiration for creative minds.

In conclusion, Barfleur stands as a jewel on the Normandy coast, inviting travelers to savor the simplicity of village life intertwined with a rich maritime history. Whether strolling along the harbor, exploring medieval streets, or savoring the flavors of the sea, every moment in Barfleur is a journey through time and a celebration of the enduring spirit of this enchanting village.

4.   Pays d'Auge

The Pays d'Auge, nestled in the heart of Normandy, France, is a region that captivates visitors with its picturesque landscapes, charming villages, and rich cultural heritage. This idyllic area, known for its rolling hills, apple orchards, and half-timbered houses, offers a serene escape from the hustle and bustle of modern life.

As one explores the Pays d'Auge, it becomes evident that this region is a tapestry of natural beauty and historic significance. The lush green countryside, adorned with grazing cattle and dotted with apple trees, creates a tranquil setting that seems to belong to a bygone era. Villages in the Pays d'Auge, such as Beuvron-en-Auge and Cambremer, showcase the quintessential Norman architecture, with charming cobblestone streets and timber-framed houses that exude timeless charm.

A defining feature of the Pays d'Auge Is its connection to the production of Calvados, an apple brandy that has achieved international acclaim. The apple orchards that blanket the landscape contribute to the production of this iconic beverage, and visitors can delve into the art of distillation by touring local distilleries. These visits offer a sensory journey, allowing guests to witness the meticulous process of turning apples into the golden elixir that is Calvados.

In addition to its culinary delights, the Pays d'Auge boasts a rich historical tapestry. Nestled amid the green hills are medieval manor houses, each with its own story to tell. These structures, often surrounded by well-tended gardens, stand as a testament to the region's historical importance and architectural prowess.

The Pays d'Auge is also home to several churches that showcase the region's religious and artistic heritage. The Saint-Pierre-sur-Dives Abbey, with its Romanesque architecture, is a prime example. Visitors can marvel at the intricate details of the abbey and immerse themselves in the spiritual ambiance that has graced the region for centuries.

As one meanders through the Pays d'Auge, the landscape unfolds like a carefully crafted painting. The Norman hedgerows, an intricate network of shrubs and trees, create a patchwork of fields that change colors with the seasons. In spring, the apple blossoms blanket the orchards in delicate hues, while autumn brings a rich tapestry of red and gold as the apples ripen.

The culinary scene in the Pays d'Auge is a celebration of local produce. From creamy Camembert to buttery croissants, the region's gastronomy is deeply rooted in tradition. Visitors can savor these delights at local markets, where farmers proudly display their fresh produce, and in quaint bistros that offer a taste of authentic Norman cuisine.

The Pays d'Auge is not merely a destination; it is an experience that engages the senses and nourishes the soul. Whether strolling through the vibrant markets, sipping Calvados in a centuries-old distillery, or simply basking in the tranquility of the countryside, visitors to this enchanting region find themselves immersed in the timeless beauty and cultural richness of the Pays d'Auge. It is a place where the past and present coexist harmoniously, inviting all who visit to become part of its story.

Lisieux

Lisieux, a quaint and spiritually significant town nestled in the heart of Normandy, France, beckons visitors with its rich history, charming architecture, and profound religious heritage. As you stroll through the cobbled streets and explore the various landmarks, you'll find yourself immersed in a unique blend of cultural and spiritual experiences.

The town is perhaps best known for its association with Saint Thérèse of Lisieux, a revered Catholic saint often referred to as "The Little Flower." The Basilica of Saint Thérèse, an architectural masterpiece dedicated to her memory, is a focal point for pilgrims and tourists alike. The basilica's stunning design and intricate details make it a must-visit destination for those interested in religious history and architecture.

Beyond the spiritual aspects, Lisieux offers a tapestry of cultural and historical attractions that captivate the imagination. The town's roots can be traced back to ancient times, and its architecture reflects a harmonious blend of medieval and Renaissance influences.

As you wander through Lisieux's charming streets, you'll encounter timber-framed houses with flower-filled balconies, creating a picturesque scene that transports you back in time. The architecture, characterized by its half-timbered structures, stands as a testament to the town's enduring heritage.

Lisieux's historic significance is further enhanced by landmarks such as the Saint-Pierre Cathedral. This Gothic masterpiece, with its soaring spires and intricate detailing, provides a glimpse into the town's medieval past. The cathedral's interior is equally impressive, housing religious artifacts and artwork that tell the story of Lisieux's cultural evolution.

For those seeking a deeper understanding of Lisieux's cultural and historical roots, a visit to the local museums is a must. The Musée d'Art et d'Histoire, housed in the Bishop's Palace, showcases an extensive collection of art and artifacts that span different periods in Lisieux's history. From ancient artifacts to Renaissance paintings, the museum offers a comprehensive overview of the town's cultural tapestry.

Lisieux is not merely a repository of the past; it is a living town with a vibrant atmosphere. The lively markets, where locals gather to sell fresh produce and handmade crafts, provide a glimpse into the daily life of Lisieux's residents. The aromas of freshly baked bread and the vibrant colors of locally sourced fruits and vegetables create a sensory experience that enhances your exploration of the town.

As the day unfolds, consider taking a leisurely stroll along the River Touques, which meanders through Lisieux's picturesque landscape. The serene riverbanks offer a tranquil escape from the hustle and bustle of daily life, providing an ideal setting for reflection and relaxation.

Culinary enthusiasts will find Lisieux to be a delightful destination. The town's restaurants and cafes serve up a delectable array of Norman cuisine, featuring locally sourced ingredients. From creamy Camembert cheese to savory apple-based dishes, the gastronomic offerings reflect the region's agricultural bounty.

A visit to Lisieux is incomplete without exploring its surroundings, which boast rolling hills, orchards, and charming villages. The Normandy countryside, with its patchwork of green fields and apple orchards, provides a serene backdrop for those seeking a respite from urban life.

Lisieux, with its spiritual allure, architectural treasures, and cultural richness, invites visitors to embark on a journey of discovery. Whether you are drawn by religious pilgrimage, historical exploration, or a desire to experience the authentic charm of a French town, Lisieux unfolds its wonders in a way that leaves a lasting impression on all who have the privilege of exploring its streets and landmarks.

5. Calvados

Calvados, a region in northwestern France, is a captivating destination that seamlessly blends history, culture, and natural beauty. Nestled within the larger region of Normandy, Calvados is known for its charming villages, picturesque landscapes, and, of course, the world-famous apple brandy that shares its name.

The landscape of Calvados is a patchwork of rolling hills, lush orchards, and quaint seaside towns. As you traverse the region, you'll encounter the distinctive half-timbered houses that are characteristic of Normandy's architecture. These structures, with their timber frames and thatched roofs, exude a timeless charm that transports visitors to a bygone era.

One of the crown jewels of Calvados is the enchanting town of Honfleur. Situated at the mouth of the Seine River, Honfleur is a picturesque port town that has inspired artists for centuries.

The Vieux Bassin, or Old Harbor, is the heart of the town, surrounded by colorful buildings that reflect in the calm waters. Honfleur's Sainte-Catherine Church, with its unique twin naves, and the cobbled streets of the historic quarter add to the town's irresistible allure.

Moving inland, the countryside of Calvados unfolds in a tapestry of apple orchards and dairy farms. The region's fertile land is not only responsible for the apples that go into making Calvados brandy but also for the production of delectable local cheeses. A leisurely drive through the countryside allows you to appreciate the beauty of the orchards in different seasons, from the blossoms of spring to the bountiful apple harvest in autumn.

The apple, however, takes on a different form of significance In Calvados – that of a key ingredient in the production of the renowned Calvados brandy. The process of making Calvados is an art that has been perfected over generations. Local distilleries, many of them family-owned, carefully select and blend apples to create this distinctive spirit. The aging process in oak barrels imparts depth and character, resulting in a beverage that is enjoyed both locally and internationally.

Deauville, another gem in the Calvados crown, offers a stark contrast to the tranquility of Honfleur. This glamorous seaside resort is synonymous with luxury, hosting film festivals, horse races, and attracting the well-heeled from around the world. The iconic Planches boardwalk, lined with beach cabins named after Hollywood stars, is a symbol of Deauville's chic allure.

Calvados is not just a feast for the eyes; it's also a culinary delight. The region's cuisine is a celebration of fresh, local produce. Seafood from the English Channel, creamy Camembert cheese, and, of course, the ubiquitous apples find their way into the kitchens of Calvados. Savoring a meal in a traditional Norman restaurant, you'll likely encounter dishes that showcase the region's gastronomic heritage.

Exploring Calvados wouldn't be complete without delving into its rich history. The region has witnessed pivotal moments, from the medieval era to the events of World War II. The remnants of ancient fortifications, such as the Château de Falaise, stand as silent witnesses to the passage of time. Museums and historical sites, like the Pegasus Bridge Museum, provide insight into the role Calvados played during the D-Day landings.

The rural tranquility and coastal elegance of Calvados make It a haven for those seeking a slower pace of life. Quaint villages like Barfleur, with its cobbled streets and medieval charm, offer a glimpse into the authentic Norman way of life. The proximity of the Cotentin Peninsula adds to the diversity of experiences, with rugged coastlines and hidden coves waiting to be discovered.

In conclusion, Calvados is a treasure trove of experiences, where history, culture, and nature intertwine to create a destination that appeals to every traveler. Whether you're strolling through the charming streets of Honfleur, sipping Calvados in a rustic distillery, or simply

basking in the tranquility of the countryside, Calvados invites you to savor the essence of Normandy. It's a region that captures the imagination, leaving an indelible mark on those fortunate enough to explore its enchanting landscapes and embrace its warm hospitality.

Honfleur: A Tapestry of Charm and Maritime Beauty

Nestled on the southern bank of the Seine estuary in the Calvados department of Normandy, Honfleur stands as a timeless gem that has captured the hearts of artists, travelers, and admirers of maritime beauty for centuries. This picturesque harbor town, with its cobblestone streets, half-timbered houses, and vibrant waterfront, exudes a unique blend of history, culture, and artistic inspiration.

Honfleur's maritime legacy dates back to the 11th century when it was a crucial port for trade and exploration. Its strategic location made it a hub for merchant ships, and the town flourished economically. Over the years, Honfleur has witnessed a rich tapestry of historical events, from medieval trade to the impressionist movement that found inspiration in its scenic landscapes.

The Vieux Bassin, or Old Harbor, is the heartbeat of Honfleur. Lined with colorful buildings that reflect in the calm waters, this iconic harbor has been immortalized in countless paintings and photographs. The sight of fishing boats gently bobbing in the harbor creates a postcard-perfect scene that encapsulates the town's maritime character.

As you wander through the narrow streets of Honfleur's historic center, you'll encounter timber-framed houses that seem frozen in time. The Sainte-Catherine Church, a remarkable structure entirely made of wood, stands as a testament to the town's medieval roots. Its separate bell tower and charming architecture add to the town's unique character.

Artistic inspiration flows through Honfleur's veins, evident in its many galleries and studios. The town has been a muse for artists such as Claude Monet, Eugène Boudin, and Johan Jongkind. The Honfleur School of Painting, a precursor to the Impressionist movement, was founded here, and the town continues to attract artists from around the world.

Beyond its artistic allure, Honfleur offers a delightful culinary experience. Quaint cafés and seafood restaurants along the waterfront serve fresh catches from the sea, including the renowned Normandy oysters. The mingling aromas of seafood, crepes, and the distinct scent of the sea create an intoxicating ambiance that enhances the overall sensory experience.

Venturing outside the town center, visitors can explore the Jardin des Personnalités, a peaceful garden that pays tribute to famous figures associated with Honfleur. From composers to writers,

each statue tells a story, adding a touch of cultural richness to the natural beauty that surrounds it.

Honfleur's charm extends to its annual events and festivals. The Honfleur Jazz Festival, held every year, transforms the town into a musical haven, attracting jazz enthusiasts and artists from near and far. The Fête de la Crevette, a celebration of shrimp and seafood, is another lively event that showcases the town's maritime bounty.

For those seeking panoramic views of Honfleur and the surrounding landscapes, a visit to the Saint-Léonard Chapel is a must. Perched on a hill, this historical chapel offers breathtaking vistas of the town, the Seine estuary, and the picturesque Normandy countryside.

Honfleur's allure is not limited to daylight hours. The town takes on a magical quality in the evening when the lights along the Vieux Bassin reflect in the water, creating a romantic atmosphere. The rhythmic sounds of footsteps on cobblestone streets, the distant murmur of conversations in waterfront cafes, and the occasional clinking of glasses contribute to the town's enchanting nightlife.

In conclusion, Honfleur stands as a testament to the enduring appeal of coastal towns that seamlessly blend history, art, and natural beauty. Its charming streets, bustling harbor, and artistic legacy create an immersive experience for visitors. Whether you're an art enthusiast, a history buff, or someone seeking a tranquil retreat by the sea, Honfleur welcomes you with open arms, promising an unforgettable journey through time and aesthetics.

Deauville: A Tapestry of Elegance, Seaside Splendor, and Cultural Riches

Nestled along the shores of the English Channel, Deauville stands as a testament to timeless elegance and refined allure. This sophisticated seaside resort, located in the Normandy region of France, has long been a beacon of glamour, drawing in visitors with its pristine beaches, upscale boutiques, and world-class amenities. As we embark on a journey through the narrative of Deauville, we unveil a tapestry woven with threads of history, cultural richness, and the sheer beauty that defines this jewel of the French coast.

The story of Deauville begins In the 19th century when the Duke of Morny, half-brother of Emperor Napoleon III, envisioned a luxurious escape for Parisian high society. The creation of Deauville, with its wide avenues, grand hotels, and a beautiful boardwalk, reflected the

opulence of the era. Over the years, Deauville evolved into a playground for the elite, frequented by artists, aristocrats, and celebrities seeking respite from urban life.

Central to the allure of Deauville is its immaculate beach, stretching for two kilometers along the coast. The golden sands, meticulously groomed and framed by iconic beach umbrellas, provide a canvas for relaxation and leisure. Locals and tourists alike indulge in sunbathing, beach games, and refreshing dips in the Channel's cool waters.

The Deauville Promenade des Planches, a charming boardwalk dating back to 1923, is a symbol of the town's glamour. With beachside cabins dedicated to famous actors and directors who have attended the annual American Film Festival, the Planches exude a nostalgic Hollywood charm. As you stroll along this historic boardwalk, the echoes of the past mingle with the laughter of the present, creating a unique ambiance.

Deauville's reputation as a luxury destination is further exemplified by its world-class hotels. The Hôtel Barrière Le Normandy, with its half-timbered façade and elegant rooms, is a classic example of Norman architecture blended with opulent hospitality. Visitors can also experience the timeless charm of the Hôtel du Golf Barrière, nestled amidst lush greenery with views of the Deauville-La Touques racecourse.

The town's casino, inaugurated in 1912, is another iconic landmark. A dazzling display of lights and a hub of entertainment, the Casino Barrière de Deauville offers a sophisticated atmosphere for gaming enthusiasts. Beyond the tables, it hosts concerts, shows, and events that contribute to the vibrant cultural scene of Deauville.

Art and culture thrive in Deauville, evident in its numerous galleries and cultural spaces. The Villa Strassburger, a stunning Norman-style mansion, houses an art collection and offers insight into the town's history. Deauville's International Centre, designed by Brazilian architect Oscar Niemeyer, is a modern testament to the town's commitment to the arts.

For equestrian enthusiasts, Deauville is synonymous with horse racing. The Deauville-La Touques racecourse, inaugurated in 1864, hosts prestigious events, including the Deauville American Film Festival and the Prix de l'Arc de Triomphe. The sight of thoroughbreds thundering down the track, against the backdrop of the sea, is a spectacle that encapsulates the town's sporting and social legacy.

Culinary delights abound in Deauville, with its restaurants offering a blend of Norman gastronomy and international cuisine. Fresh seafood, particularly oysters and mussels, takes center stage, accompanied by the region's renowned apple-based products, such as Calvados and cider. Deauville's gourmet scene invites visitors to savor exquisite flavors while enjoying panoramic views of the sea.

As the sun sets over Deauville, the town takes on a magical glow. The iconic Casino lights up, and the beachfront becomes a romantic tableau. Deauville's nightlife offers a mix of sophistication and entertainment, with bars, clubs, and beachfront lounges providing diverse options for those seeking evening enjoyment.

In conclusion, Deauville is more than a destination; it is an experience steeped in history, elegance, and a sense of timelessness. Whether you seek the glamour of high-end boutiques, the tranquility of a beachside retreat, or the excitement of cultural events, Deauville welcomes you with open arms. This coastal haven, where luxury meets tradition, invites you to become part of its narrative—a narrative that continues to captivate hearts and imaginations with each passing tide.

CHAPTER 2: EXPLORING HISTORICAL AND CULTURAL RICHES IN NORMANDY

Mont Saint-Michel

Address: Le Mont Saint-Michel, 50170 Mont-Saint-Michel, France

One of the most iconic landmarks not just in Normandy but in the whole of France, Mont Saint-Michel is a medieval abbey perched on a rocky island. Its gothic architecture and the surrounding bay create a mesmerizing scene. Visitors can explore the abbey, stroll through the narrow streets of the village, and witness the spectacular tidal changes that make the island accessible during low tide.

D-Day Landing Beaches

Address (Omaha Beach): Omaha Beach, 14710 Vierville-sur-Mer, France

The D-Day Landing Beaches hold immense historical significance, marking the site of the Allied invasion during World War II. Omaha Beach, in particular, witnessed intense fighting on June 6, 1944. Visitors can explore the beaches, visit museums and memorials, and gain a profound understanding of the sacrifices made during this pivotal moment in history.

Normandy American Cemetery

Address: Normandy American Cemetery, Omaha Beach, 14710 Colleville-sur-Mer, France

Adjacent to Omaha Beach, the Normandy American Cemetery is a poignant reminder of the lives lost during the D-Day landings. The immaculately kept cemetery is the final resting place for thousands of American soldiers. The site evokes deep emotions, offering a space for reflection and remembrance.

Bayeux Tapestry

Address: Bayeux Tapestry Museum, 13B Rue de Nesmond, 14400 Bayeux, France

The Bayeux Tapestry is an extraordinary piece of medieval art that narrates the events leading up to the Norman Conquest of England. Displayed in a museum in the town of Bayeux, this 70-

meter-long embroidered cloth is a UNESCO-listed cultural treasure, providing a unique window into the history of the region.

Château de Falaise

Address: Château de Falaise, 14700 Falaise, France

For a journey back in time, visit the Château de Falaise. This fortress played a crucial role in the medieval history of Normandy and is famously known as the birthplace of William the Conqueror. The castle, perched on a high crag, offers panoramic views and a glimpse into the medieval way of life.

Saint-Étienne-du-Mont Abbey

Address: Abbaye Saint-Étienne-du-Mont, Place Sainte-Geneviève, 50200 Coutances, France

Nestled in the charming town of Coutances, the Saint-Étienne-du-Mont Abbey is a masterpiece of Norman Romanesque architecture. Dating back to the 11th century, the abbey boasts stunning stained glass windows and intricately carved sculptures, making it a haven for history and art enthusiasts.

Normandy's historical and cultural attractions offer a rich tapestry of experiences, from the medieval splendor of Mont Saint-Michel to the somber reflections at the Normandy American Cemetery. Each site narrates a unique chapter in the region's history, providing visitors with a profound appreciation for Normandy's cultural heritage.

Mont Saint-Michel: A Marvel of Medieval Architecture and Spiritual Grandeur

Perched majestically on a rocky islet in Normandy, France, Mont Saint-Michel stands as a testament to the ingenuity of medieval architecture and the enduring spirit of human creativity. This iconic island commune, crowned by its stunning abbey, is not only a visual spectacle but also a site of historical and cultural significance that draws millions of visitors each year.

Mont Saint-Michel's history dates back to the 8th century when, according to legend, the Archangel Michael appeared to Bishop Aubert of Avranches, instructing him to build a church

on the rocky islet. Over the centuries, this humble beginning evolved into the breathtaking abbey and village that we see today.

The approach to Mont Saint-Michel is as enchanting as the destination itself. As visitors traverse the causeway during low tide or take a shuttle during high tide, the silhouette of the abbey gradually reveals itself against the backdrop of the bay. The scene is nothing short of magical, transporting visitors to a bygone era where knights and monks roamed the cobblestone streets.

Upon reaching the island, visitors are greeted by a labyrinth of narrow alleys and stone houses, creating an otherworldly atmosphere. The architecture, with its medieval charm, offers a glimpse into the daily life of the monks and villagers who once inhabited this unique commune. As you ascend towards the abbey, the view becomes increasingly panoramic, revealing the vastness of the bay and the surrounding landscape.

The abbey itself is a masterpiece of medieval construction. Built over multiple levels, it seems to defy gravity as it reaches towards the heavens. The abbey's spires and turrets rise against the sky, creating a silhouette that is both imposing and ethereal. The Gothic and Romanesque architectural elements showcase the skill of the craftsmen who toiled over centuries to create this spiritual sanctuary.

Venturing inside the abbey, visitors are treated to a wealth of historical and religious artifacts. The Abbey Church, with its soaring ceilings and intricate stained glass windows, is a hymn to the divine. The Crypt, located beneath the church, adds an extra layer of mystique, inviting contemplation in the dim light. The Refectory, where the monks once dined, and the Knights' Room, adorned with coats of arms, provide glimpses into the daily life of the religious community.

The Abbey's cloisters, with their delicate columns and serene gardens, offer a tranquil escape. Walking through these cloisters, one can almost feel the presence of the monks who sought solace in these hallowed halls. The views from the ramparts, overlooking the bay and the changing tides, provide a breathtaking panorama that captivates the soul.

Mont Saint-Michel is not merely a static monument frozen in time; it's a living testament to the ebb and flow of history. It has weathered wars, witnessed the passage of kings and conquerors, and stood resilient against the elements. The strategic location of Mont Saint-Michel made it an impregnable fortress during times of conflict, adding another layer of historical significance to its narrative.

Beyond its architectural and historical splendor, Mont Saint-Michel has also inspired countless artists, writers, and poets. Its ethereal beauty has been captured in paintings and described in prose, immortalizing its allure in the realm of creativity. The interplay of light and shadow on the abbey's façade, especially during sunrise or sunset, creates a canvas that transcends the boundaries of mere stone and mortar.

The surrounding bay of Mont Saint-Michel is a UNESCO World Heritage site, renowned for its dramatic tidal variations. The sight of the tide rushing in to isolate the island or receding to reveal the causeway is a natural spectacle that adds a dynamic element to the visitor's experience. The bay is also a haven for birdwatchers, with various seabirds and migratory species finding refuge in its tranquil waters.

In recent years, efforts have been made to preserve and protect Mont Saint-Michel and its fragile ecosystem. Sustainable tourism practices and conservation initiatives aim to ensure that future generations can continue to marvel at this jewel of Norman heritage.

Mont Saint-Michel is not merely a destination; it's a pilgrimage through time and space. It beckons travelers to step into a world where the spiritual and the earthly converge, where history is etched into the very stones, and where the beauty of nature complements the achievements of human craftsmanship. Whether seen from a distance or explored up close, Mont Saint-Michel is an enduring symbol of human aspiration and the enduring power of architectural marvels. It invites us to reflect on the passage of time, the interplay of cultures, and the indomitable spirit that has shaped this extraordinary monument.

The Echoes of History: A Journey Through Normandy's D-Day Landing Beaches

June 6, 1944—the date etched in history as D-Day, the day that marked the largest seaborne invasion in history and a pivotal turning point in World War II. On the windswept shores of Normandy, the D-Day Landing Beaches stand as silent witnesses to the valor, sacrifice, and determination of thousands of Allied soldiers. In this expansive essay, we embark on a journey through the hallowed grounds of Omaha, Utah, Gold, Juno, and Sword Beaches, exploring the indelible marks left by the events of that fateful day.

Normandy, with its serene landscapes and picturesque coastal towns, bears the scars of a tumultuous past. However, it is these very scars that narrate a tale of liberation, resilience, and the unyielding spirit of humanity. The beaches, once stained with the blood of the fallen, are now places of reflection, remembrance, and homage to the heroes who gave their all for the cause of freedom.

Omaha Beach

Omaha Beach, codenamed "Easy Red," witnessed some of the fiercest fighting on D-Day. As the American forces stormed the shore, they faced formidable German defenses that turned the beach into a deadly battleground. Today, the expansive stretch of sand and the imposing bluffs overlooking the sea serve as a stark reminder of the price paid for liberty. Visitors can walk along the shoreline, imagining the chaos and heroism that unfolded in the face of adversity.

Utah Beach

Utah Beach, the westernmost landing point, was chosen for its relative ease of access. Yet, the unexpected challenges posed by the marshy terrain and German fortifications tested the resolve of the invading forces. Exploring Utah Beach today, with its museums and memorials, allows visitors to grasp the intricacies of the amphibious assault and appreciate the strategic decisions that shaped the course of the battle.

Gold Beach

Gold Beach, assigned to the British forces, played a critical role in securing the eastern flank of the invasion. As troops landed under heavy fire, they faced the daunting task of neutralizing enemy defenses. The remnants of Mulberry Harbor, an ingenious engineering feat to facilitate the unloading of troops and supplies, still stand testament to the ingenuity and determination that defined the D-Day landings.

Juno Beach

Juno Beach, assigned to Canadian forces, witnessed intense fighting as soldiers faced a formidable German defense. The stories of bravery and sacrifice on Juno Beach are immortalized in the monuments and cemeteries that dot the landscape. Exploring this beach offers a profound understanding of the multinational effort that defined the liberation of Europe.

Sword Beach

Sword Beach, the easternmost landing point, marked the intersection of British and Free French forces. The successful capture of this beach paved the way for the liberation of Caen and

beyond. Today, Sword Beach is a place of quiet contemplation, where the echoes of the past linger in the sea breeze.

As we traverse the D-Day Landing Beaches, it becomes evident that these shores are not mere geographical locations; they are living testaments to the human cost of war and the triumph of the human spirit. The cemeteries that grace the landscape, such as the Normandy American Cemetery and the Canadian Cemetery at Bény-sur-Mer, are poignant reminders of the individuals who made the ultimate sacrifice.

The museums that dot the coastline, such as the Utah Beach Museum and the Juno Beach Centre, offer immersive experiences, showcasing artifacts, personal accounts, and multimedia presentations that transport visitors back to that historic day. The exhibits not only chronicle the military strategies and tactics but also shed light on the individual stories of courage and camaraderie that unfolded on these shores.

Normandy's D-Day Landing Beaches, now places of pilgrimage for history enthusiasts and veterans alike, evoke a profound sense of gratitude and humility. The tangible scars on the landscape—the remnants of bunkers, the pockmarked cliffs, and the rusting hulks of landing craft—serve as a living tableau of the tumultuous events that unfolded on that decisive day.

The legacy of D-Day extends beyond the beaches themselves. The nearby towns and villages, which played integral roles in the logistics and support of the invasion, offer a glimpse into the resilience of the local population. The church in Sainte-Mère-Église, forever associated with the paratrooper caught on its steeple, and the Pegasus Bridge, a symbol of airborne operations, are integral parts of this tapestry of history.

In conclusion, the D-Day Landing Beaches of Normandy are not just historical sites; they are sacred grounds that embody the ideals of freedom, democracy, and the enduring human spirit. As we walk in the footsteps of the soldiers who landed on these beaches, we are reminded that the lessons of the past are not to be forgotten but cherished, for it is through understanding our history that we pave the way for a more peaceful future.

I.   Omaha Beach: The Heart of Valor and Sacrifice in Normandy

Normandy, a region of France celebrated for its picturesque landscapes and charming coastal towns, carries a profound weight of history. Amidst its serene beauty lies a stretch of shoreline that resonates with a somber but heroic tale – Omaha Beach. On June 6, 1944, this seemingly

tranquil expanse of sand became the crucible of courage and the theater of indomitable human spirit. In this comprehensive exploration, we delve into the depths of Omaha Beach, uncovering the stories of bravery, the echoes of gunfire, and the enduring legacy of one of the most significant chapters in World War II.

Omaha Beach, codenamed "Easy Red" during the D-Day landings, occupies a pivotal place in the collective memory of those who have studied the history of World War II. On that fateful day, the American forces faced a formidable challenge as they landed on this stretch of the Normandy coastline. What ensued was a battle of unimaginable intensity – a struggle for the very freedom that we cherish today.

To truly understand the significance of Omaha Beach, we must transport ourselves back to that summer morning in 1944. The air was thick with tension as Allied troops embarked on a mission of unprecedented scale. The success of Operation Overlord depended on the swift and secure establishment of beachheads, and Omaha Beach was at the forefront of this monumental endeavor.

The beach stretches for about five miles along the English Channel, with its golden sands juxtaposed against high bluffs that seemed to defy the invading forces. The plan was to land infantry and armored divisions, establish a beachhead, and then push inland to secure vital objectives. However, the German defenses were far more formidable than anticipated, transforming the shores of Omaha Beach into a battleground of unimaginable chaos.

The formidable Atlantic Wall, a complex network of fortifications built by the German forces, awaited the approaching Allied forces. Pillboxes, bunkers, and trenches embedded in the cliffs provided the German defenders with a strategic advantage. As the American soldiers waded through the cold waters towards the shore, they were met with a withering hail of gunfire. Many landing craft were destroyed before they could reach the beach, and those that made it faced an onslaught that would be etched in history.

The carnage on Omaha Beach was overwhelming. Soldiers, weighed down by equipment and struggling against the elements, faced a barrage of bullets and artillery fire. The beach was stained with the blood of the fallen, and the air resonated with the cries of the wounded. In the face of seemingly insurmountable odds, the resolve of the Allied forces was tested to its limits.

The story of Omaha Beach is not just one of tragedy; it is a testament to the unparalleled bravery displayed by the American soldiers that day. Despite the chaos, soldiers pressed forward, storming the beach with unwavering determination. Leaders emerged from the chaos, rallying their troops and adapting to the evolving situation. Officers like Brigadier General Norman Cota and non-commissioned officers displayed extraordinary courage, leading their men under intense fire.

The first hours on Omaha Beach were critical, and the tenacity of the American forces eventually led to the establishment of a precarious foothold. The surviving soldiers fought their way up the bluffs, overcoming the odds stacked against them. By the end of the day, the beach was secured, but the cost was immense. Casualties were staggering, and the landscape was forever altered by the scars of war.

Today, as one stands on the shores of Omaha Beach, the weight of history is palpable. The expansive beach, now a place of serenity, bears witness to the tumultuous events of that summer day. The remnants of the Atlantic Wall, the bunkers that once housed German defenders, and the occasional rusting hulk of landing craft serve as silent monuments to the ferocity of the battle.

The Normandy American Cemetery and Memorial, overlooking Omaha Beach, stands as a testament to the sacrifice of those who gave their lives. Row upon row of white crosses and Stars of David, meticulously aligned on the manicured lawn, evoke a profound sense of gratitude and humility. The cemetery, with its chapel and memorial, serves as a place of solemn reflection, allowing visitors to pay their respects to the fallen.

The stories of Individual heroism at Omaha Beach are as diverse as the men who fought that day. From medics administering aid under fire to soldiers dragging their wounded comrades to safety, each account adds a layer of humanity to the narrative of war. The "Bedford Boys," a group of young men from the small town of Bedford, Virginia, suffered disproportionately high casualties on D-Day, highlighting the impact of war on communities.

The landscape around Omaha Beach Is dotted with monuments and memorials, each telling a unique aspect of the story. The Vierville Draw, the site of intense fighting, is marked by the Les Braves sculpture, a soaring tribute to the spirit of freedom. The Dog Green sector, where the first waves of assault faced the fiercest resistance, is now a place of quiet contemplation. The monuments, such as the National Guard Monument and the Big Red One Assault Museum, offer insights into the experiences of specific units during the battle.

Omaha Beach, in its current state of tranquility, belies the tumultuous events that unfolded on its shores nearly eight decades ago. The sea breeze carries whispers of the past, and the rhythmic waves seem to echo the footsteps of those who landed on its sands. The cliffs, once a fortress against the invaders, now stand as silent sentinels, guarding the memories of the fallen.

The legacy of Omaha Beach extends beyond its historical significance. It serves as a poignant reminder of the cost of freedom and the responsibilities that come with it. The D-Day landings were not just a military campaign; they were a collective endeavor to preserve the values that we hold dear. The courage displayed on Omaha Beach transcends national boundaries, reminding us that the pursuit of freedom is a universal aspiration.

As we reflect on the events of D-Day and the significance of Omaha Beach, it becomes evident that the stories of heroism and sacrifice are not confined to the pages of history books. They live on in the collective consciousness of nations and resonate in the hearts of those who visit these sacred grounds. Omaha Beach, with its scars and stories, stands as a beacon of hope and a testament to the resilience of the human spirit in the face of adversity.

In conclusion, Omaha Beach is more than a geographical location; it is a symbol of courage, sacrifice, and the enduring quest for freedom. As we stand on its shores, we are not just observers of history but participants in the ongoing narrative of human perseverance. The echoes of D-Day, carried by the winds that sweep across Omaha Beach, serve as a reminder that the pursuit of a better world is a responsibility shared by all.

II.   Utah Beach: A Hallowed Shoreline of Sacrifice and Triumph

June 6, 1944—the day that would forever alter the course of history. On the windswept shores of Normandy, Utah Beach became a theater of courage, sacrifice, and triumph. Codenamed "Utah," this stretch of coastline witnessed the convergence of strategy, bravery, and the indomitable human spirit. In this exploration, we delve into the profound significance of Utah Beach, unraveling the events of D-Day and the enduring legacy imprinted on this hallowed shoreline.

Utah Beach, situated on the westernmost edge of the D-Day Landing sites, was assigned to the United States forces as a crucial point of entry into German-occupied France. The selection of Utah Beach was strategic; its topography offered relative ease of access compared to the other beaches, making it a key target for the Allied forces seeking to establish a secure beachhead.

As dawn broke on June 6, 1944, the sea off Utah Beach roared with the thunder of naval bombardments. The initial assault, primarily carried out by the U.S. 4th Infantry Division, faced the daunting challenge of navigating through a treacherous landscape. The Normandy coastline, characterized by marshy terrain and a complex system of German defenses, posed formidable obstacles to the invading forces.

The success of the Utah Beach landing was not without challenges. Unforeseen factors, such as strong currents and navigational errors, led to the landing craft being dispersed over a wider area than anticipated. This dispersion, while initially posing confusion, turned out to be a stroke of luck, as it led to a more decentralized German defense and contributed to the overall success of the Utah Beach operation.

The early hours of the assault saw soldiers storming the beaches under heavy fire. The struggle to establish a beachhead was intense, and the bravery displayed by the troops was nothing short of heroic. Overcoming the challenges of hostile fire and the natural obstacles of the landscape, the Allied forces fought inch by inch to secure Utah Beach.

One of the key elements contributing to the success of the Utah Beach landing was the deployment of the specialized "Higgins boats." Designed to navigate shallow waters, these landing craft played a pivotal role in delivering troops and equipment to the beach. The ingenuity of the amphibious assault, with its combination of naval, air, and ground forces, showcased the collaborative and multifaceted nature of Operation Overlord.

Utah Beach, once a battlefield strewn with the remnants of war, is now a place of reflection and remembrance. The Utah Beach Museum stands as a testament to the events of that historic day. Situated near the landing site, the museum offers a comprehensive portrayal of the D-Day landings, with exhibits featuring artifacts, personal accounts, and immersive displays that transport visitors back to the harrowing hours of June 6, 1944.

The artifacts on display at the Utah Beach Museum range from personal belongings of soldiers to the machinery used in the amphibious assault. Each item tells a story—a story of individuals who faced the unknown with courage and conviction. The museum, with its meticulous curation, serves as a bridge connecting the present to the past, ensuring that the legacy of Utah Beach endures for generations to come.

Adjacent to the museum lies the Utah Beach Cemetery, a final resting place for the brave soldiers who gave their lives on that fateful day. The serene rows of white crosses stand in solemn tribute, a poignant reminder of the human cost of freedom. The nearby sculpture, "Les Braves," further symbolizes the spirit of those who landed on Utah Beach, with its soaring wings representing the rise from oppression to liberty.

Beyond the museum and cemetery, the landscape of Utah Beach itself bears witness to the events of D-Day. The bunkers, craters, and remnants of fortifications scattered along the shoreline serve as silent sentinels, preserving the scars of war. Exploring the beach, one can almost hear the echoes of the past—the shouts of soldiers, the rumble of tanks, and the distant thunder of naval bombardments.

Utah Beach, beyond its historical significance, is a place of pilgrimage for veterans, their families, and history enthusiasts from around the world. The annual commemorations on June 6th draw people together to pay homage to the courage of those who fought on this beach. The presence of surviving veterans, now frail with age but resolute in spirit, adds a deeply poignant dimension to these ceremonies.

In addition to the formal monuments and memorials, Utah Beach is marked by the simple yet powerful traces of history. The pillboxes, gun emplacements, and other remnants of German defenses stand as stark reminders of the challenges faced by the Allied forces. The landscape, shaped by the scars of conflict, is a canvas on which the story of Utah Beach unfolds.

The legacy of Utah Beach extends beyond its role in World War II. It serves as a symbol of the enduring alliance between the United States and France and the shared commitment to the values of freedom and democracy. The beach, once a battleground, is now a symbol of reconciliation and friendship between nations.

Utah Beach, with its somber beauty, invites contemplation on the nature of war, the resilience of the human spirit, and the responsibilities that come with freedom. As we stand on this hallowed shoreline, we are reminded that the lessons of history are not confined to the pages of books; they are etched in the sands of Utah Beach, where the echoes of the past continue to resonate. The footprints left by those who landed here, imprinted in the soil and in our collective memory, guide us toward a future where the sacrifices of the past are honored, and the pursuit of peace remains paramount.

III. *Gold Beach: Echoes of Valor, Sands of Liberation*

In the annals of history, certain places emerge as crucibles of courage, sacrifice, and resilience. Gold Beach, nestled along the Normandy coast, is such a place. Its name resonates with the echoes of the past, conjuring images of soldiers storming the shore under a hail of gunfire, determined to change the course of history. In this expansive exploration, we delve into the sands of Gold Beach, uncovering the tales of bravery, the strategic brilliance, and the indomitable spirit that defined this crucial juncture of World War II.

Before the dawn of June 6, 1944, Gold Beach was a tranquil stretch of coastline, its serene beauty belying the impending storm of war. Tasked with the mission of the 50th (Northumbrian) Infantry Division and elements of the 8th Armoured Brigade, Gold Beach stood as a linchpin in the Allied plan to liberate Western Europe.

Strategic considerations played a pivotal role in the selection of Gold Beach. Its proximity to the vital port of Arromanches, where the ingenious Mulberry Harbour would be constructed, made it a linchpin in the logistical chain of the invasion. The success of the landings at Gold Beach was essential for establishing a secure beachhead and facilitating the swift movement of troops and supplies.

As dawn broke on that fateful day, the waters off Gold Beach became a theater of war. The initial assault involved a combination of amphibious landings, airborne operations, and naval bombardments. The soldiers of the 50th Division and supporting units, many of whom were part of the British Army, faced a daunting task as they navigated through beach obstacles and German defenses.

The challenges were multifaceted. From the underwater obstacles designed to impede landing craft to the fortified positions along the coast, the defenders were prepared to repel any attempt at an amphibious assault. The success of the operation hinged on the ability of the Allied forces to breach these defenses swiftly and establish a secure foothold on the beach.

Despite the challenges, the Allied forces exhibited remarkable valor and tenacity. The infantry, supported by specialized units and armor, moved inland, gradually securing the beachhead. The construction of the Mulberry Harbour at Arromanches commenced, a testament to the meticulous planning that went into ensuring the success of the invasion.

Gold Beach, once a battleground, transformed into a bustling hub of activity. Troops disembarked, supplies were unloaded, and the logistical machinery of war began to turn. The success at Gold Beach contributed significantly to the overall success of Operation Overlord, setting the stage for the liberation of France and the eventual defeat of Nazi Germany.

The legacy of Gold Beach extends far beyond the events of June 6, 1944. Today, the sands that bore witness to the struggle for freedom are places of remembrance, reflection, and reverence. The remnants of the Mulberry Harbour, though weathered by time and the elements, stand as tangible monuments to human ingenuity and the collaborative effort that defined the Allied victory.

Cemeteries, such as the Bayeux War Cemetery, are solemn grounds that pay tribute to the lives lost during the assault on Gold Beach and the subsequent campaign. Rows of white crosses and Stars of David stand in silent homage to the soldiers who made the ultimate sacrifice.

Visitors to Gold Beach today are greeted by a landscape that blends the tranquility of the sea with the echoes of history. Museums, such as the Gold Beach Museum at Arromanches, provide a comprehensive understanding of the events that transpired on D-Day. Artifacts, personal accounts, and interactive exhibits offer a poignant and educational experience.

The remnants of German bunkers, coastal defenses, and the poignant sculptures that dot the coastline serve as reminders of the intense struggles that unfolded on these shores. Exploring the beach, one can almost hear the echoes of the past—the rumble of tanks, the staccato of machine gun fire, and the shouts of command.

Gold Beach stands as a bridge between the past and the present—a place where the sands of liberation absorbed the blood, sweat, and tears of a generation. The valor displayed on this beach, the sacrifices made, and the strategic brilliance that unfolded have left an indelible mark on the pages of history.

As we tread lightly on the sands of Gold Beach today, it is incumbent upon us to remember not only the events of June 6, 1944, but the ideals for which those brave soldiers fought. Gold Beach is not merely a location; it is a sacred space that beckons us to reflect on the cost of freedom and to honor the legacy of those who paved the way for a brighter future.

IV. Juno Beach

Juno Beach, etched into history as one of the pivotal sites of the D-Day landings on June 6, 1944, stands as a testament to courage, sacrifice, and the indomitable human spirit. As we delve into the rich tapestry of Juno Beach, we uncover the stories of heroism, the strategic importance of this coastal stretch, and the lasting impact it has left on the landscape and the collective memory of a generation.

The early morning of June 6, 1944, saw the skies above Juno Beach filled with the deafening roar of aircraft engines as Allied forces embarked on a daring mission to liberate Western Europe from the grip of Nazi occupation. Situated along the Normandy coast, Juno Beach was assigned to the Canadian forces as part of Operation Overlord, the largest amphibious assault in history.

Canadian soldiers, drawn from across the vast expanse of their nation, found themselves in the vanguard of the assault on Juno Beach. Their objective was clear but daunting: to establish a beachhead, secure vital strategic points, and pave the way for the liberation of France and, ultimately, Europe.

The beaches of Normandy, with their golden sands and tranquil beauty, bore witness to a violent clash of ideologies on that fateful day. Juno Beach, a 10-kilometer stretch of coastline between Courseulles-sur-Mer and Saint-Aubin-sur-Mer, became a theater of war where the fate of nations hung in the balance.

The coastal defenses were formidable, with the German forces well-prepared to repel any attempted invasion. Concrete bunkers, machine gun nests, and obstacles submerged beneath the waves awaited the Canadian soldiers as they approached the shore in the early hours of June 6. The element of surprise was compromised, and the beachhead became a killing ground as machine gun fire and artillery barrages rained down on the advancing troops.

Yet, in the face of overwhelming adversity, the Canadian forces displayed remarkable bravery and resilience. The soldiers faced not only the physical obstacles of the beach but also the psychological toll of knowing that success meant pushing through the well-entrenched German defenses. The shoreline, which bore witness to the ebb and flow of the tides, now bore witness to the ebb and flow of human courage.

Juno Beach was not just a battleground; it was a crucible that tested the mettle of those who landed on its shores. The beach itself, once serene and idyllic, transformed into a landscape scarred by the ravages of war. The sand, soaked with the blood of fallen comrades, became a sacred ground where the cost of freedom was laid bare.

The assault on Juno Beach unfolded with the kind of precision that belied the chaos and carnage on the ground. The Canadian soldiers faced stiff resistance but pressed on, capturing key objectives and paving the way for the subsequent phases of the Normandy campaign. The town of Courseulles-sur-Mer, situated at the western end of Juno Beach, was a crucial target that needed to be secured to ensure the success of the overall operation.

As we traverse the sands of Juno Beach today, the remnants of that historic day are still visible. The concrete bunkers, now weathered and worn, stand as silent sentinels to the past. They are not just structures of concrete and steel; they are relics that whisper the stories of the soldiers who fought and died on this stretch of coastline.

The Juno Beach Centre, located in Courseulles-sur-Mer, serves as a living memorial to the Canadian contribution to the Allied victory. The museum, with its immersive exhibits and personal narratives, provides visitors with a profound understanding of the events that unfolded on D-Day. It is not just a repository of artifacts; it is a bridge that connects the past with the present, ensuring that the sacrifices made on Juno Beach are not consigned to the fading pages of history.

Walking through the Juno Beach Centre, visitors are confronted with the faces of the men who landed on these shores. Photographs, letters, and personal effects evoke a sense of intimacy with those who faced the horrors of war. The exhibits, meticulously curated, transport visitors back to that pivotal moment in history, allowing them to experience, if only vicariously, the challenges and triumphs of the Canadian forces on D-Day.

The landscape around Juno Beach, while now serene and picturesque, bears the subtle scars of conflict. The town of Courseulles-sur-Mer, once a battleground, has risen from the ashes to become a thriving community. The harbor, which witnessed the arrival of Canadian troops on D-Day, now bustles with fishing boats and yachts. It is a testament to the resilience of the human spirit and the capacity to rebuild even in the aftermath of profound tragedy.

The Canadian Cemetery at Bény-sur-Mer, situated near Juno Beach, is a place of solemn reflection. Rows upon rows of white gravestones, meticulously aligned, pay homage to the soldiers who made the ultimate sacrifice. The tranquility of the cemetery, overlooking the English Channel, belies the tumultuous history that brought these men to this hallowed ground.

Juno Beach, with its stories of valor and sacrifice, is not just a historical site; it is a living memorial that demands contemplation and reverence. The stretch of coastline, where the tide of history turned in favor of the Allied forces, invites visitors to reflect on the fragility of peace and the enduring price of freedom.

As the years pass and the veterans of D-Day become fewer, the responsibility to remember and honor their legacy falls to each new generation. The ceremonies held on Juno Beach, particularly on anniversaries of D-Day, draw people from around the world. The sight of Canadian flags fluttering in the sea breeze, juxtaposed against the serene backdrop of the beach, is a poignant reminder of the enduring bonds forged in the crucible of war.

In conclusion, Juno Beach is a sacred space that transcends the boundaries of time. It is a place where history and memory intersect, inviting us to walk in the footsteps of those who faced the crucible of war with unwavering resolve. As we stand on the sands of Juno Beach, we are not just witnesses to history; we are participants in a collective journey of remembrance and gratitude. The echoes of the past reverberate through the waves, reminding us that the freedoms we cherish today were secured through the sacrifices made on this hallowed ground.

V. Sword Beach: A Tapestry of History, Sacrifice, and Liberation

June 6, 1944—D-Day. The mere mention of this date evokes images of heroism, sacrifice, and the turning tide of World War II. Among the five landing beaches on the Normandy coast, Sword Beach stands as a testament to the multinational effort that unfolded on that historic day. As we delve into the intricacies of Sword Beach, we uncover a tapestry of history woven with the threads of valor, strategy, and the pursuit of liberty.

Stretching along the easternmost flank of the Normandy invasion, Sword Beach was assigned to British and Free French forces. Its strategic significance lay in its proximity to the crucial city of Caen, a linchpin in the German defense. The planning and execution of the Sword Beach assault were fraught with challenges, yet the Allied forces embarked on this mission with a singular determination—to breach the Atlantic Wall and begin the liberation of Western Europe.

The beach, a seemingly serene stretch of sand, belies the tumultuous events that unfolded on that fateful day. The invasion began with the landing of airborne troops in the early hours of June 6. Paratroopers from the 6th Airborne Division descended from the night sky, aiming to secure key objectives and disrupt German defenses. The iconic Pegasus Bridge, captured in a daring glider assault, became a symbol of the successful airborne operations that preceded the beach landings.

As the sun rose on the morning of D-Day, the horizon off Sword Beach became a panorama of ships, landing craft, and the distant hum of aircraft. The sea, usually a symbol of tranquility, transformed into a theater of war as Allied forces approached the French coast. The amphibious assault on Sword Beach commenced, with infantry divisions, tanks, and supporting units landing under a hail of German gunfire.

The oppositeion was formidable. German bunkers and fortifications lined the coast, and seasoned troops of the German 716th Infantry Division were prepared to repel the invaders. The first wave of Allied troops faced a barrage of obstacles, both natural and man-made. Mines, barbed wire, and machine gun nests created a lethal labyrinth that the soldiers had to navigate under fire.

The success of the Sword Beach assault was contingent on the rapid capture of key objectives, including the town of Ouistreham and the pivotal city of Caen. The British 3rd Infantry Division and the Free French forces faced fierce resistance but pressed forward with unwavering determination. The town of Ouistreham fell into Allied hands, and the push toward Caen commenced.

The capture of Pegasus Bridge and the liberation of Ouistreham were critical milestones, but the real test lay in the ability to penetrate deeper into enemy territory. Caen, a major road and rail hub, became a focal point of the Normandy campaign. The Battle for Caen, marked by intense urban combat, would persist for weeks, but the success at Sword Beach set the stage for the eventual liberation of the city.

Amidst the chaos of war, moments of individual heroism and camaraderie shone brightly. The bravery of the soldiers who stormed the beaches, the ingenuity of the engineers who cleared obstacles, and the resilience of the medical teams treating the wounded—all these elements coalesced into a symphony of collective effort.

The landscape of Sword Beach today bears the scars of that historic day. The remnants of German bunkers, the pockmarked cliffs, and the rusting hulks of landing craft serve as tangible reminders of the fierce struggle that unfolded here. The beach, once stained with the blood of the fallen, is now a place of pilgrimage for those seeking to pay homage to the heroes who sacrificed for the cause of freedom.

The story of Sword Beach extends beyond the shoreline. The nearby town of Ouistreham, once a battleground, now thrives as a symbol of post-war reconstruction. The museums and memorials that dot the area, such as the Ouistreham-Riva Bella Grand Bunker Museum and the Hillman Fortress, offer immersive experiences that transport visitors back to that pivotal moment in history.

The Commonwealth War Graves Cemetery at Hermanville-sur-Mer and the French War Cemetery at Riva-Bella stand as solemn reminders of the human cost of war. Rows upon rows of white crosses and gravestones, meticulously maintained, tell the stories of lives cut short but not forgotten. The peacefulness of these cemeteries, overlooking the sea, contrasts sharply with the tumultuous events that unfolded on the beaches below.

In the decades since D-Day, Sword Beach has become a symbol of reconciliation and friendship. The international cooperation that led to the liberation of Normandy paved the way for a new era of collaboration among nations. The Twinning of Cities program, which fosters connections between cities in the United Kingdom and France, exemplifies the enduring bonds forged in the crucible of war.

As we reflect on the significance of Sword Beach, we recognize that its legacy extends far beyond the events of June 6, 1944. It is a landscape that encapsulates the complexities of war— the valor of the soldiers, the challenges of strategy, and the human toll. Sword Beach, with its echoes of history, stands as a testament to the triumph of the human spirit over adversity.

In conclusion, Sword Beach invites us to tread upon its shores not merely as a historical site but as sacred ground where the aspirations for freedom were translated into action. The stories of courage and sacrifice that unfolded here continue to resonate, urging us to remember the past, honor the fallen, and strive for a world where the lessons of history guide us toward lasting peace.

Normandy American Cemetery

In the heart of Normandy, where the waves of the English Channel gently caress the shores, lies a hallowed ground that echoes with the solemnity of sacrifice and the valor of those who fought for freedom. The Normandy American Cemetery, situated near the historic Omaha Beach, stands as a poignant testament to the courage and sacrifice of the men who landed on the beaches of Normandy on June 6, 1944 – a day that would become eternally engraved in the annals of history as D-Day.

Nestled on a cliff overlooking the vast expanse of Omaha Beach, the Normandy American Cemetery is a sacred resting place for over 9,300 American soldiers who gave their lives during the Normandy campaign of World War II. The cemetery's immaculate white crosses and Stars of David stand in solemn rows, each representing an individual who played a crucial role in the liberation of Europe from the grip of tyranny.

The sheer scale of the Normandy American Cemetery is overwhelming, stretching over 170 acres of meticulously maintained grounds. As one approaches the entrance, the sheer magnitude of the sacrifice becomes evident. The rows upon rows of white marble crosses, perfectly aligned, create a visual testament to the magnitude of the operation and the price paid for freedom.

Each grave, whether marked by a cross or a Star of David, represents a story – a life cut short in the prime of its existence. The meticulous care given to the grounds and the pristine condition of each marker convey a profound sense of respect and honor for the fallen. The cemetery's design, with its gentle slopes and carefully manicured lawns, creates an atmosphere of serenity and reverence.

The central feature of the Normandy American Cemetery is the iconic Memorial, a semicircular structure constructed with gleaming Portland stone. The memorial bears the names of over 1,500 servicemen whose final resting places are unknown or were lost at sea. From this vantage point, visitors can gaze out over Omaha Beach, the same beach that witnessed the ferocious battles and heroic acts that defined D-Day.

The Memorial's walls are adorned with a powerful mosaic map depicting the Allied landings in Normandy. This mosaic serves as a visual narrative, allowing visitors to trace the footsteps of those who fought and perished for the cause of liberty. The names inscribed on the walls are a reminder that, behind every statistic, lies an individual with dreams, hopes, and aspirations – a person whose sacrifice contributed to shaping the course of history.

The Normandy American Cemetery Is not merely a burial ground; it is a living memorial that pays homage to the spirit of camaraderie and shared sacrifice. The Memorial Plaza, adorned with sculptures and inscriptions, invites contemplation and reflection. A bronze statue, titled "The Spirit of American Youth Rising from the Waves," serves as a symbolic representation of the indomitable spirit that rose from the chaos of war.

As visitors wander through the cemetery, they encounter poignant moments of reflection at the gravesites. The personal inscriptions on the markers, often chosen by the families, reveal glimpses of the personalities and passions of the departed. Flowers, flags, and mementos left by visitors are a testament to the ongoing connection between the living and the fallen.

Every year, the Normandy American Cemetery attracts countless visitors from around the world who come to pay their respects and to remember. Veterans, family members, and history enthusiasts gather to honor the sacrifices made by these brave men. The annual commemorative events, particularly on the anniversary of D-Day, infuse the air with a sense of gratitude and remembrance.

The Normandy American Cemetery's significance extends beyond its role as a burial ground. It is an educational institution, a place where the lessons of history are etched into the minds of those who walk its solemn paths. School groups, scholars, and individuals seeking to understand the impact of war on a personal level find themselves drawn to this sacred ground.

The Visitor Center, adjacent to the cemetery, serves as a gateway to a deeper understanding of the events that transpired on D-Day and the ensuing Battle of Normandy. Exhibits, artifacts, and multimedia presentations provide a comprehensive overview of the largest amphibious assault in history. The center's mission is not only to commemorate the past but also to educate future generations about the cost of freedom.

One cannot help but be moved by the photographs, letters, and personal effects on display at the Visitor Center. These artifacts humanize the historical narrative, offering a glimpse into the lives of the men who fought and perished on the beaches of Normandy. The narratives of courage, fear, and camaraderie come alive, creating a bridge between the past and the present.

Beyond its historical and educational significance, the Normandy American Cemetery serves as a symbol of international unity and collaboration. The graves of the fallen represent not only American servicemen but also soldiers from various Allied nations who stood shoulder to shoulder in the fight against tyranny. The international flags that flutter alongside the Stars and Stripes at the entrance underscore the collaborative effort that defined the liberation of Europe.

The Normandy American Cemetery and Memorial stands as a living tribute to the principles for which these men gave their lives – freedom, democracy, and the defense of human dignity. It is a place where the enormity of the sacrifice is met with the enduring spirit of hope and resilience. The cemetery's serene beauty, coupled with its historical weight, transforms it into a sacred space where visitors can contemplate the fragility of peace and the resilience of the human spirit.

In conclusion, the Normandy American Cemetery is more than a memorial; it is a sacred landscape that embodies the indomitable spirit of those who faced the crucible of war. As visitors walk through its hallowed grounds, they are reminded that freedom is not free – it is a gift bestowed upon us by the valor and sacrifice of those who came before. The Normandy American Cemetery beckons us to remember, to honor, and to ensure that the echoes of D-Day reverberate through the corridors of history, inspiring generations to come.

The Bayeux Tapestry: A Tapestry of History

In the small town of Bayeux, nestled in the picturesque region of Normandy, France, lies a cultural treasure that transcends time—the Bayeux Tapestry. This remarkable piece of medieval art, measuring approximately 70 meters in length, is an embroidered cloth that unfolds a narrative of historical significance. As visitors step into the Bayeux Tapestry Museum, they are transported back to a pivotal moment in history, immersing themselves in the events that led to the Norman Conquest of England.

The Bayeux Tapestry is not, in fact, a true tapestry but an embroidery—a distinction that adds to its allure. Created in the 11th century, the tapestry is believed to have been commissioned by Bishop Odo of Bayeux, the half-brother of William the Conqueror. Its creation is often attributed to a team of skilled embroiderers who meticulously stitched scenes onto a linen canvas.

The entire narrative unfolds in a continuous strip, creating a visual epic that tells the story with vivid detail. The scenes are accompanied by Latin inscriptions, providing a narrative thread that guides viewers through the historical tale. The Bayeux Tapestry is divided into various sections, each depicting different episodes of the story.

The narrative commences with the promise of Harold, Earl of Wessex, to support William of Normandy's claim to the English throne. The intricate embroidery captures the moment when Harold is shipwrecked and subsequently taken captive by Count Guy of Ponthieu. This event sets the stage for the unfolding drama that culminates in the Battle of Hastings.

As the story progresses, viewers witness the preparations for the Battle of Hastings, one of the defining moments in English history. The depiction of the Battle of Hastings is particularly captivating, showcasing the chaos and intensity of medieval warfare. The scene captures the death of Harold, famously depicted with an arrow piercing his eye—a detail that has become an iconic symbol of the tapestry.

Beyond the military aspects, the Bayeux Tapestry also provides glimpses into the daily life and customs of the time. Scenes of feasting, hunting, and other activities offer a nuanced portrayal of the medieval world. The tapestry serves as a visual historical document, shedding light on the clothing, architecture, and weaponry of the era.

Despite its age, the Bayeux Tapestry has remarkably survived the ravages of time. Its preservation is a testament to the craftsmanship of its creators and the careful custodianship it has received over the centuries. The tapestry was displayed in Bayeux Cathedral for much of its history until it found a permanent home in the Bayeux Tapestry Museum in the late 20th century.

The Bayeux Tapestry is more than an artistic masterpiece—it is a key source for understanding the events leading up to the Norman Conquest. Historians and scholars have scrutinized its details to glean insights into the political, military, and cultural aspects of the time. The tapestry serves as a primary source that provides valuable clues about the mindset and perspectives of the individuals involved in these historical events.

In addition to its historical significance, the Bayeux Tapestry is a work of art that continues to captivate audiences with its intricate design and storytelling prowess. The vibrant colors, the expressive characters, and the dynamic compositions make it a living tableau that brings history to life. Visitors to the Bayeux Tapestry Museum have the unique opportunity to stand in front of this medieval marvel, absorbing the details and nuances that make it a cultural gem.

The Bayeux Tapestry's journey through time has not been without controversy and debate. Questions about its origins, purpose, and the accuracy of its historical account have fueled scholarly discussions for centuries. The mystery surrounding the tapestry adds an element of intrigue, inviting visitors to contemplate the motivations behind its creation and the messages it seeks to convey.

As a UNESCO-listed cultural treasure, the Bayeux Tapestry continues to draw admirers from around the world. Its enduring legacy extends beyond the borders of Normandy, transcending cultural and linguistic barriers. The tapestry has become a symbol of the shared history of England and Normandy, a tangible link to a momentous chapter that shaped the destinies of these lands.

In conclusion, the Bayeux Tapestry is a masterful testament to the intertwining of art and history. It invites visitors to embark on a visual journey through the events that shaped the fate of nations. In the quiet town of Bayeux, this extraordinary piece of embroidery stands as a living witness to the past, a tapestry that speaks across the centuries, ensuring that the echoes of history are not forgotten.

Château de Falaise: A Storied Fortress on the Cliffs

Perched majestically atop the rugged cliffs of Normandy, Château de Falaise stands as a silent witness to centuries of history. This imposing fortress, with its soaring towers and commanding presence, has played a pivotal role in the medieval narrative of Normandy and, by extension, the broader history of France. From its strategic vantage point, Château de Falaise has not only witnessed the ebb and flow of battles but has also been intimately linked to the lives of some of the most influential figures in European history.

The origins of Château de Falaise can be traced back to the 10th century. Strategically positioned on a high crag, the castle served as a defensive stronghold, protecting the town of Falaise and the surrounding region. Its construction was initiated by William the Conqueror's father, Robert the Magnificent, and completed by William himself. The castle's robust fortifications and

innovative architectural features made it an impregnable bastion, a testament to the military prowess of its builders.

One of the most significant chapters in Château de Falaise's history is its association with William the Conqueror. Born within the castle walls in 1028, William went on to become one of the most formidable rulers of his time. The influence of Château de Falaise on William's formative years is undeniable, and the castle stands as a tangible link to the roots of the Norman Conquest of England in 1066.

Château de Falaise is a marvel of medieval architecture. The complex comprises a series of structures, including the keep, inner bailey, and outer bailey. The keep, with its sturdy stone walls and defensive towers, dominates the skyline. Exploring the interior of the castle is like stepping back in time, with narrow passageways, hidden chambers, and atmospheric courtyards evoking the spirit of medieval life.

The strategic importance of Château de Falaise cannot be overstated. Its elevated position provided a vantage point for surveilling the surrounding landscape, enabling its occupants to detect potential threats from a considerable distance. The castle's role in regional defense was pivotal during times of conflict, including the Hundred Years' War and the Wars of Religion.

Over the centuries, Château de Falaise underwent various modifications and renovations, reflecting the evolving nature of military architecture. From its early days as a feudal fortress to its adaptation as a Renaissance residence, the castle's architectural evolution mirrors the broader changes in the political and social landscape of Normandy.

Beyond its military significance, Château de Falaise is a repository of cultural heritage. The castle houses exhibits and displays that offer visitors a glimpse into the daily life of medieval inhabitants. Artifacts, armor, and period reconstructions contribute to a rich tapestry of historical storytelling, making a visit to Château de Falaise not merely a tour of stone walls but a journey into the heart of Norman history.

As with any castle with centuries of history, Château de Falaise has its share of legends and tales. From stories of hidden treasure within its walls to tales of ghostly apparitions haunting its corridors, the castle's mystique adds an extra layer of intrigue for those who delve into its history.

Today, Château de Falaise welcomes visitors from around the world to explore its storied halls and battlements. The panoramic views from the castle provide a breathtaking panorama of the

Norman countryside, inviting reflection on the castle's enduring role in shaping the destiny of the region.

In conclusion, Château de Falaise stands not only as a physical testament to medieval fortification but as a living chronicle of the turbulent history of Normandy. Its towers echo with the footsteps of knights, the whispers of political intrigue, and the dreams of a young William the Conqueror. A visit to Château de Falaise is an immersive journey through time, offering a profound connection to the rich cultural heritage of this remarkable fortress on the cliffs of Normandy.

Saint-Étienne-du-Mont Abbey

Saint-Étienne-du-Mont Abbey stands as a testament to the enduring beauty of Norman Romanesque architecture and the rich cultural heritage that defines the heart of France. Nestled in the picturesque town of Coutances, this abbey is a historical treasure that has weathered the tides of time, its stone walls echoing with the whispers of centuries.

The abbey's origins trace back to the 11th century, a period marked by the confluence of architectural innovation and religious fervor. Construction commenced in 1030 under the auspices of Bishop Geoffroy de Montbray, a figure whose vision and dedication would see the rise of an edifice that would capture the essence of medieval spirituality.

As one approaches Saint-Étienne-du-Mont Abbey, the eye is drawn to the soaring spires and the harmonious blend of Romanesque and Gothic elements. The façade, adorned with intricate carvings and sculptures, tells the silent story of the skilled craftsmen who lent their artistry to this sacred space. Each stone seems to bear witness to the passage of time, yet retaining a timeless elegance that captivates the beholder.

Upon crossing the threshold, visitors are immersed in an atmosphere of profound tranquility. The nave, with its high vaulted ceilings and graceful arches, creates a sense of awe, inviting contemplation and reflection. The play of light through the stained glass windows bathes the interior in a kaleidoscope of colors, casting a mesmerizing glow upon the worn stone floor.

The abbey's architectural layout reflects the spiritual aspirations of its creators. The transept, with its crossing tower, symbolizes the intersection of the earthly and the divine. Chapels dedicated to saints, each adorned with unique sculptures and decorations, provide intimate spaces for prayer and meditation.

A focal point of Saint-Étienne-du-Mont Abbey is its choir, a space reserved for the monastic community's sacred rituals. The intricately carved choir stalls, dating back to the 18th century, are a testament to the craftsmanship of the era. These wooden masterpieces depict scenes from biblical narratives, adding a layer of narrative depth to the sacred space.

The abbey's history has not been without its challenges. Over the centuries, Saint-Étienne-du-Mont has undergone several renovations and restorations, each phase leaving its mark on the architectural canvas. The abbey, despite the passage of wars, revolutions, and the inexorable march of time, has stood resilient, a guardian of cultural and spiritual continuity.

The organ, a majestic instrument positioned in the choir loft, resonates through the abbey, filling the sacred space with music that transcends temporal boundaries. The echoes of hymns and chants, which have reverberated through these stone walls for centuries, contribute to the immersive experience of visitors, connecting them to the spiritual tapestry woven by generations past.

As one explores the abbey's surroundings, the exterior reveals a cloister—a serene courtyard enclosed by covered walkways. This architectural feature served both practical and contemplative purposes for the monks who once inhabited the abbey. The cloister, adorned with delicate columns and arches, provides a tranquil haven where the whispers of the wind carry the echoes of centuries-old prayers.

Saint-Étienne-du-Mont Abbey is not merely a relic of the past; it continues to play a vital role in the cultural life of Coutances. Regular religious services, concerts, and cultural events breathe life into the ancient stones, ensuring that the abbey remains a vibrant hub for both spiritual and artistic expression.

For those who seek a deeper understanding of the abbey's history and significance, the attached museum offers a curated collection of artifacts, manuscripts, and artworks. Each piece contributes to the narrative of Saint-Étienne-du-Mont, allowing visitors to trace the threads of its storied past.

The abbey's location within Coutances adds to its allure. The town, with its cobblestone streets and medieval charm, provides a fitting backdrop for this architectural gem. Visitors can wander through the quaint squares, savoring the ambiance of a town where history and modernity coexist in harmonious balance.

In conclusion, Saint-Étienne-du-Mont Abbey is more than a historical monument; it is a living testament to the enduring spirit of Norman culture and religious heritage. Its walls, adorned with the artistry of centuries, invite visitors to step into a world where time seems to stand still, and the echoes of the past resonate with a timeless melody. This abbey, with its architectural splendor and cultural richness, stands as a beacon, guiding those who enter to a deeper appreciation of the intertwining threads of history and spirituality.

CHAPTER 3: OUTDOOR ADVENTURES

Hiking and Walking Trails in Normandy: A Nature Lover's Paradise

Normandy, with its picturesque landscapes and diverse terrain, offers a plethora of hiking and walking trails for nature enthusiasts and adventure seekers. Whether you're a seasoned hiker or someone looking for a leisurely stroll amidst nature, Normandy has something to offer for everyone. In this guide, we'll explore some of the most captivating trails, providing not only breathtaking views but also a chance to immerse yourself in the rich history and culture of the region.

1. *Mont Saint-Michel Bay Trail*

Location: Mont Saint-Michel, Normandy

Distance: 6 miles

Difficulty: Moderate

Embark on a journey along the stunning bay of Mont Saint-Michel. This trail not only offers panoramic views of the iconic Mont Saint-Michel but also takes you through salt marshes and past ancient medieval structures. Starting near the Mont Saint-Michel causeway, the trail winds its way through the bay, providing a unique perspective of this UNESCO World Heritage site.

2. *GR21 – Alabaster Coast*

Location: Etretat to Le Havre

Distance: 50 miles

Difficulty: Challenging

For the avid hiker seeking a challenge, the GR21 trail along the Alabaster Coast is a must-try. Stretching from the famous cliffs of Etretat to the bustling port city of Le Havre, this trail offers

breathtaking views of towering cliffs, pebble beaches, and charming seaside villages. Be prepared for steep ascents and descents, but the stunning scenery along the way makes it all worthwhile.

3. Forest of Brotonne Loop

Location: Brotonne Forest

Distance: 8 miles

Difficulty: Easy to Moderate

Escape into the tranquility of Brotonne Forest with this delightful loop trail. The trail takes you through ancient woodlands, along the Seine River, and past charming villages. It's an ideal choice for those looking for a peaceful walk surrounded by nature. Keep an eye out for local wildlife, and don't forget to bring a picnic to enjoy by the river.

4. D-Day Landing Beaches Trail

Location: Utah Beach to Omaha Beach

Distance: 5 miles

Difficulty: Easy

Step back in time as you walk along the historic D-Day landing beaches. Starting at Utah Beach and winding its way to Omaha Beach, this trail is not only a scenic walk along the coastline but also a poignant journey through World War II history. Visit the various memorials and museums along the way, paying homage to the bravery of the soldiers who landed on these shores.

5. Suisse Normande – The Orne Valley

Location: Clecy

Distance: 10 miles

Difficulty: Moderate

Discover the beauty of Suisse Normande as you hike through the picturesque Orne Valley. The trail takes you through lush green landscapes, past charming villages, and offers stunning views of the meandering river below. This is a great option for those looking for a varied terrain, with forests, hills, and riverbanks all in one hike.

Normandy's hiking and walking trails are a treasure trove for nature lovers and history enthusiasts alike. From the iconic Mont Saint-Michel to the historic D-Day landing beaches, each trail offers a unique blend of natural beauty and cultural richness. Lace up your hiking boots, grab a map, and get ready to explore the breathtaking landscapes of Normandy on foot.

Remember to respect nature, follow trail guidelines, and immerse yourself fully in the serenity that these trails provide.

Happy hiking!

Mont Saint-Michel Bay Trail

Nestled in the heart of Normandy, the Mont Saint-Michel Bay Trail stands as a testament to the region's natural beauty and historical significance. This trail, spanning approximately 6 miles, weaves through the captivating landscapes surrounding the iconic Mont Saint-Michel, offering hikers a unique and immersive experience.

As you embark on this enchanting journey, the trail begins near the Mont Saint-Michel causeway. This vantage point provides a breathtaking first glimpse of the medieval abbey perched on the rocky island. The panoramic view from here sets the tone for the adventure that awaits, promising a blend of natural wonders and cultural richness.

The Mont Saint-Michel Bay Trail, with its moderate difficulty level, caters to a wide range of hikers, making it accessible to both novices and seasoned trekkers. The terrain varies from well-maintained paths to more rugged sections, ensuring a diverse and engaging hiking experience.

One of the highlights of this trail is the opportunity to traverse the vast bay during low tide. This unique aspect allows hikers to witness the tidal flats, revealing an otherworldly landscape of sandbanks and channels. The vastness of the bay, coupled with the distant silhouette of Mont Saint-Michel, creates a surreal atmosphere that leaves a lasting impression.

As you venture further along the trail, you'll find yourself immersed in the natural wonders of the bay ecosystem. The salt marshes, with their unique flora and fauna, provide a glimpse into the ecological diversity of this coastal region. Birdwatchers will particularly appreciate the presence of various seabirds, adding a touch of wildlife to the hiking experience.

The trail meanders through landscapes that have witnessed centuries of history. Ruins of old mills and remnants of medieval structures dot the route, serving as silent witnesses to the

changing tides of time. This integration of historical elements into the natural environment creates a harmonious blend, enhancing the cultural significance of the Mont Saint-Michel Bay Trail.

For those seeking a deeper connection with the history of the region, interpretive signs along the trail provide valuable insights into the cultural and historical context of Mont Saint-Michel and its surroundings. Hikers can learn about the abbey's construction, the bay's tidal phenomena, and the role of Mont Saint-Michel in various historical events.

Photographers, too, will find the Mont Saint-Michel Bay Trail a treasure trove of opportunities. The ever-changing play of light and shadow on the abbey, the reflections in the tidal pools, and the wide vistas of the bay offer countless picturesque moments. Each turn in the trail reveals a new perspective, beckoning shutterbugs to capture the essence of this magical landscape.

As you approach Mont Saint-Michel itself, the trail unveils the intricate details of this architectural marvel. The awe-inspiring abbey, with its soaring spires and medieval charm, stands as a testament to human ingenuity and perseverance. Hikers can explore the narrow streets of the village surrounding the abbey, absorbing the atmosphere of this UNESCO World Heritage site.

Timing is crucial when undertaking the Mont Saint-Michel Bay Trail, especially if you wish to experience the ethereal beauty of the bay during low tide. Planning your hike to coincide with this natural spectacle adds an extra layer of wonder to the journey, allowing you to traverse the exposed seabed and witness the gradual reveal of the ancient paths leading to Mont Saint-Michel.

In conclusion, the Mont Saint-Michel Bay Trail is a mesmerizing expedition that seamlessly blends nature, history, and culture. Whether you're drawn to the historical significance of Mont Saint-Michel, the diverse ecosystems of the bay, or the sheer joy of hiking in a picturesque setting, this trail promises an unforgettable adventure. Lace up your hiking boots, embrace the rhythm of the tides, and immerse yourself in the enchanting beauty of Mont Saint-Michel and its bay.

GR21 - Alabaster Coast

The GR21, tracing the Alabaster Coast of Normandy, is a spectacular hiking trail that stretches for about 50 miles from the famous cliffs of Etretat to the vibrant port city of Le Havre. This trail is not only a feast for the avid hiker seeking a challenge but also a visual delight for anyone who appreciates stunning landscapes and coastal views.

Starting at the iconic cliffs of Etretat, the GR21 takes you on a journey along some of the most breathtaking scenery in Normandy. The trail meanders along the Alabaster Coast, named for the chalk cliffs that dominate the shoreline. These cliffs, with their striking white color, create a dramatic contrast with the deep blue waters of the English Channel, providing a visual spectacle that is both awe-inspiring and unforgettable.

The trail is known for its challenging terrain, characterized by steep ascents and descents. Hikers should be prepared for a workout, but the rewards are well worth the effort. As you navigate the undulating path, you'll be treated to panoramic views of the cliffs, the sea, and the picturesque countryside.

One of the highlights of the GR21 is the opportunity to explore the charming seaside villages that dot the coastline. These villages, with their traditional architecture and quaint charm, provide a welcome respite for hikers. Strolling through these coastal communities allows you to immerse yourself in the local culture, perhaps sampling fresh seafood at a seaside café or interacting with friendly locals.

Throughout the hike, you'll encounter a variety of natural landscapes, from pebble beaches to rugged cliffs to lush green meadows. The diversity of the terrain adds to the allure of the GR21, ensuring that every step brings a new and captivating vista. The trail is also rich in flora and fauna, offering opportunities for nature enthusiasts to spot local plant and animal species along the way.

The 'R21 is not just a physical challenge; it's also a journey through history. The coastline of Normandy played a pivotal role in World War II, and remnants of this history are visible along the trail. Hikers can explore bunkers and other military structures, gaining insight into the region's wartime past. This historical dimension adds a layer of depth to the hiking experience, making it more than just a scenic walk.

As the trail approaches Le Havre, hikers are treated to the sight of a bustling port city. Le Havre, a UNESCO World Heritage site, is known for its modernist architecture and vibrant cultural scene. The GR21 concludes in this dynamic city, allowing hikers to explore its museums, galleries, and waterfront areas. It's a fitting end to a journey that spans natural beauty, cultural richness, and historical significance.

While the GR21 is a challenging trail, its accessibility makes it suitable for hikers with varying levels of experience. The well-maintained path is clearly marked, and there are opportunities for shorter hikes or day trips for those who prefer a less strenuous adventure. The trail also offers a range of accommodations along the way, from charming bed and breakfasts to comfortable hotels, ensuring that hikers can rest and recharge after a day of exploration.

In conclusion, the GR21 along the Alabaster Coast is a hiking experience like no other. It combines the physical challenge of a long-distance trail with the sensory delights of stunning

coastal scenery, charming villages, and a rich tapestry of history. Whether you're a seasoned hiker seeking an adventure or a nature lover looking to explore Normandy's beauty on foot, the GR21 promises an unforgettable journey along one of Europe's most captivating coastlines.

Forest of Brotonne Loop

The Forest of Brotonne Loop, nestled In the heart of Normandy, France, is a hidden gem for nature lovers and outdoor enthusiasts. This enchanting trail spans approximately 8 miles, meandering through the ancient woodlands of Brotonne Forest, tracing the curves of the Seine River, and unveiling the beauty of charming villages along the way.

The Forest of Brotonne, also known as Forêt Domaniale de Brotonne, is one of the largest beech forests in France. Its rich biodiversity, coupled with the soothing melodies of chirping birds and rustling leaves, creates an immersive experience for those seeking solace in nature.

The trail begins its journey in the heart of Brotonne Forest, where towering trees form a natural canopy, filtering sunlight and creating a dappled effect on the forest floor. The scent of earth and moss accompanies hikers as they embark on this tranquil escapade. The Forest of Brotonne Loop is designed to provide an escape from the hustle and bustle of daily life, allowing visitors to reconnect with nature in its purest form.

As the trail winds deeper into the forest, the rhythmic crunch of leaves beneath each step becomes a melody that harmonizes with the gentle whispers of the wind. The forest floor, adorned with wildflowers and ferns, offers a vibrant tapestry of colors that change with the seasons. In spring, a carpet of bluebells stretches as far as the eye can see, while autumn transforms the landscape into a mosaic of reds, oranges, and golds.

One of the highlights of the Forest of Brotonne Loop is its proximity to the Seine River. The trail gracefully follows the riverbank, offering intermittent glimpses of the water through the dense foliage. Hikers can pause at designated viewpoints to absorb the serene beauty of the Seine as it flows gracefully, reflecting the surrounding greenery like a liquid mirror. This interaction between the forest and the river enhances the trail, providing a dynamic and ever-changing backdrop.

Along the way, the trail leads to charming villages that seem frozen in time. Quaint cottages with flower-filled gardens line the path, and the occasional village square invites hikers to rest and soak in the local atmosphere. These villages, with their rustic charm and friendly inhabitants, add a cultural dimension to the Forest of Brotonne Loop, creating a holistic experience that combines nature and heritage.

Wildlife enthusiasts will find the Forest of Brotonne to be a haven for observing native species. The forest is home to a diverse range of fauna, including deer, boar, and a variety of bird species. Hikers may encounter red squirrels darting through the trees or hear the distinctive call of the Eurasian jay echoing through the forest.

As the trail unfolds, it presents opportunities for quiet contemplation. Secluded clearings and strategically placed benches offer hikers a chance to pause, breathe in the crisp forest air, and absorb the meditative ambiance. The Forest of Brotonne Loop is not just a physical journey but an introspective one, allowing visitors to disconnect from the demands of modern life and reconnect with the rhythms of nature.

The Forest of Brotonne Loop also caters to various skill levels, making it accessible to both novice hikers and seasoned trekkers. The well-maintained trails are clearly marked, ensuring that visitors can navigate the route with ease. Interpretive signs along the way provide insights into the flora, fauna, and history of the forest, enhancing the educational value of the hike.

In conclusion, the Forest of Brotonne Loop stands as a testament to the natural beauty and cultural richness that Normandy has to offer. This trail is not merely a physical journey through the woods but a transformative experience that engages the senses and nourishes the soul. As hikers emerge from the forest canopy, they carry with them not only the memories of a scenic walk but a profound connection to the timeless beauty of the Forest of Brotonne.

D-Day Landing Beaches Trail

The D-Day Landing Beaches Trail stands as a poignant and historic testament to the valor and sacrifice of those who participated in one of the most pivotal events of World War II. Stretching along the Normandy coastline, these beaches witnessed the Allied forces' daring amphibious assault on June 6, 1944 – D-Day. The trail encapsulates not just a scenic journey along the shores but an immersive exploration of the events that unfolded on that fateful day.

As you tread on the sands of Utah Beach, there's an overwhelming sense of history seeping through the ground. This was one of the primary landing zones for the American forces. The remnants of the temporary harbors, known as Mulberries, still visible in the water, evoke a vivid image of the logistical challenges faced during the invasion.

Moving eastward, Omaha Beach beckons with its wide expanse of sand and daunting cliffs. Here, the American forces faced fierce German resistance, resulting in one of the bloodiest battles of D-Day. The Normandy American Cemetery and Memorial, overlooking the beach, stands as a solemn tribute to the thousands of soldiers who paid the ultimate price for freedom.

Gold Beach, where British forces landed, presents a different perspective. The coastal town of Arromanches-les-Bains, just off Gold Beach, is home to the remains of the Mulberry Harbour "Port Winston." The remnants of this artificial harbor, an engineering marvel of its time, offer a tangible connection to the challenges faced by the Allies in ensuring a steady flow of troops and supplies.

Juno Beach, the next in line, witnessed the Canadian forces landing alongside British units. The Juno Beach Centre, a museum and cultural center, provides a comprehensive insight into the Canadian contribution to D-Day and the subsequent battles in Normandy.

Sword Beach, the easternmost landing zone, marked the convergence of British and Free French forces. The town of Ouistreham, near Sword Beach, houses the Pegasus Bridge Museum. The capture of Pegasus Bridge by British airborne troops was a crucial prelude to the beach landings, and the museum narrates this daring feat.

The D-Day Landing Beaches Trail is not just a journey through landscapes; it's a narrative woven with tales of courage, sacrifice, and resilience. Each beach, each bunker, and each cemetery tells a story – a story of a day that changed the course of history.

Standing on these beaches today, with the sea breeze whispering through, it's hard to fathom the chaos and carnage that engulfed these shores on that summer day in 1944. The tranquility of the present sharply contrasts with the cacophony of war that once echoed here.

The bunkers, many of them still standing, are a stark reminder of the fortified German defenses that the Allies had to breach. Exploring these bunkers offers a glimpse into the strategic challenges faced by both sides during the Normandy Campaign.

One cannot discuss the D-Day Landing Beaches without acknowledging the resilience of the local population. Normandy, once a theater of war, has transformed into a region of peace and reconciliation. The hospitality of the locals is a testament to the healing power of time and the shared commitment to preserving the memory of the past.

Beyond the beaches, the airborne landings played a crucial role in securing the success of the D-Day operation. The drop zones for paratroopers and gliders, such as Sainte-Mère-Église, still echo with the echoes of those daring night missions. The Airborne Museum in Sainte-Mère-Église vividly recounts the stories of the paratroopers who descended from the night sky into the heart of enemy territory.

As you traverse the D-Day Landing Beaches Trail, it becomes apparent that this is not merely a historical excursion; it's a pilgrimage. The monuments, memorials, and cemeteries are not mere markers on a map; they are sacred spaces that demand reflection and remembrance.

The Battle of Normandy, of which D-Day was the pivotal opening act, marked a turning point in World War II. It was a collective effort, a testament to the resolve of nations united against

tyranny. The D-Day Landing Beaches Trail invites visitors to stand on the shores where this history unfolded, to walk in the footsteps of heroes, and to pay homage to those who gave everything for the cause of freedom.

In conclusion, the D-Day Landing Beaches Trail is a journey through time – a journey that evokes profound emotions and prompts deep reflection. It's a tribute to the bravery of the soldiers who stormed these beaches, the ingenuity of the commanders who devised the invasion, and the resilience of the human spirit in the face of adversity. As you walk along these hallowed shores, you can't help but feel a profound sense of gratitude for the sacrifices made and a renewed commitment to preserving the memory of those who shaped the destiny of nations on that fateful day in 1944.

Suisse Normande - The Orne Valley

Nestled in the heart of Normandy, the Suisse Normande region captivates visitors with its undulating landscapes, charming villages, and the picturesque Orne Valley. This enchanting area, often referred to as the "Swiss Normandy," offers a unique blend of natural beauty and outdoor adventures. As you embark on a journey through the Orne Valley, you'll find yourself immersed in lush greenery, meandering rivers, and a tapestry of landscapes that showcase the diversity of this hidden gem.

The Orne Valley, coursing through Suisse Normande, unveils a rich tapestry of natural wonders. A haven for outdoor enthusiasts, this region presents a myriad of opportunities for hiking, cycling, and simply basking in the serenity of the French countryside. Let's delve into the essence of Suisse Normande, tracing the contours of the Orne Valley as it weaves through this captivating landscape.

The gentle hum of the river accompanies you as you traverse the pathways along the Orne Valley. This watercourse, with its crystal-clear waters, mirrors the verdant surroundings, creating a soothing backdrop for your exploration. The banks of the Orne River are adorned with a mosaic of flora, from willow trees gracefully bowing towards the water to vibrant wildflowers that add a splash of color to the meadows.

As you venture deeper into Suisse Normande, the landscape transforms, revealing rugged hills and limestone cliffs that provide a dramatic contrast to the tranquility of the riverbanks. The Orne Valley, in its meandering course, unveils surprises at every turn—a hidden waterfall cascading down moss-covered rocks, a centuries-old stone bridge that whispers tales of bygone eras, and expansive vistas that stretch as far as the eye can see.

The trails In the Orne Valley cater to a spectrum of outdoor enthusiasts, from casual strollers to seasoned hikers seeking a more challenging ascent. The diversity of the terrain ensures that every step leads to a new discovery. Forested paths invite you to wander beneath canopies of beech and oak, the rustling leaves creating a symphony of nature's melodies. Open meadows offer panoramic views, providing the perfect setting for a leisurely picnic or a moment of quiet contemplation.

Suisse Normande is dotted with quaint villages that seem frozen in time. Charming stone houses adorned with vibrant blooms line the narrow streets, and the aroma of freshly baked bread wafts from local bakeries. The locals, with their warm hospitality, add a human touch to the natural splendor, creating an atmosphere that feels both timeless and welcoming.

One such village along the Orne Valley is Clecy, a gateway to the Suisse Normande region. Nestled between the hills, Clecy boasts a unique character that reflects the spirit of this enchanting area. The village square, with its cafes and artisan shops, invites you to linger and soak in the unhurried pace of life. From Clecy, you can embark on various trails that lead you deeper into the Suisse Normande, each promising a new perspective on the Orne Valley's beauty.

For those seeking a moderate hiking experience, the 10-mile loop trail around Clecy is a delightful choice. The trail meanders through the village, offering glimpses of its architectural heritage, before leading you into the heart of the Orne Valley. The path unfolds along the riverbanks, and as you ascend the hills, you're rewarded with breathtaking vistas of the surrounding landscape.

As you traverse the trail, you might encounter fellow adventurers—a friendly nod or exchange of greetings with like-minded explorers adds a communal spirit to the experience. The beauty of the Orne Valley lies not only in its physical grandeur but in the shared moments of awe and appreciation among those who traverse its trails.

The Orne Valley is also a haven for cyclists, with a network of biking routes that crisscross the region. Whether you're an avid mountain biker seeking rugged trails or a leisure cyclist yearning for a scenic ride, Suisse Normande accommodates all preferences. The cycling paths wind through charming hamlets, offering opportunities to pause and interact with locals who are often eager to share stories about their community and its ties to the land.

Adventure seekers can explore the more challenging aspects of Suisse Normande, including rock climbing on the limestone cliffs that characterize the region. The exhilaration of scaling these natural formations is matched only by the awe-inspiring views awaiting those who reach the summit. The cliffs not only provide a thrilling vertical adventure but also serve as vantage points from which to appreciate the intricate contours of the Orne Valley.

A particularly enchanting aspect of Suisse Normande Is its commitment to preserving its natural heritage. The trails are carefully maintained to ensure minimal impact on the environment, and responsible tourism is encouraged. This dedication to sustainability enhances the authenticity of the experience, allowing visitors to connect with the landscape in a way that respects and values its intrinsic beauty.

The changing seasons paint the Orne Valley with a kaleidoscope of colors, each offering a unique perspective on Suisse Normande's allure. In the spring, wildflowers carpet the meadows, and the budding leaves on the trees create a canopy of fresh green hues. Summer brings warmth, and the riverbanks become a popular spot for picnics and relaxation. In the fall, the landscape transforms into a tapestry of reds, oranges, and yellows as the leaves change, casting a warm glow on the trails. Winter, with its crisp air, offers a different kind of beauty, as frosty landscapes evoke a sense of quiet enchantment.

As the day draws to a close, and the sun begins its descent beyond the hills, the Orne Valley takes on a magical quality. The golden hour bathes the landscape in a soft, warm glow, casting long shadows that dance across the trails. It's a time for reflection, a moment to appreciate the simple joys of being surrounded by nature's wonders.

In conclusion, the Orne Valley in Suisse Normande is a treasure trove for those who seek a harmonious blend of natural beauty, outdoor adventure, and cultural richness. Whether you're drawn to the tranquility of a riverside walk, the challenge of a rugged hike, or the thrill of climbing limestone cliffs, Suisse Normande invites you to embark on a journey of discovery.

As you traverse the trails, breathe in the crisp air, listen to the symphony of nature, and let the Orne Valley weave its magic around you. Suisse Normande, with its timeless landscapes and welcoming villages, beckons you to explore, connect, and create lasting memories amidst the beauty of the French countryside.

Beach Activities in Normandy: A Coastal Paradise

Nestled along the rugged coastline of northern France, Normandy boasts some of the most stunning and diverse beaches in Europe. From the picturesque sands overlooking the English Channel to the historic D-Day landing beaches, Normandy offers a wealth of opportunities for beach enthusiasts. In this guide, we will explore the myriad of beach activities that make Normandy a must-visit destination for sun-seekers, history buffs, and adventure lovers alike.

1. Sun, Sand, and Serenity

Normandy's beaches are renowned for their natural beauty and tranquility. The soft, golden sands stretch for miles, providing the perfect setting for a leisurely day of relaxation. Visitors can bask in the gentle coastal breeze, soak up the sun, or take a refreshing dip in the cool waters of the English Channel. The beaches of Normandy offer a serene escape from the hustle and bustle of everyday life, making them ideal for a rejuvenating retreat.

2. Water Sports Extravaganza

For those seeking a more active beach experience, Normandy has a plethora of water sports to offer. Windsurfing and kiteboarding enthusiasts will find the brisk winds along the coast ideal for catching waves. Local surf schools provide lessons for beginners, ensuring that everyone can enjoy the thrill of riding the waves. Kayaking and paddleboarding are also popular choices, allowing visitors to explore the picturesque coves and inlets that dot the shoreline.

3. D-Day Landing Beaches: A Historical Journey

Normandy's beaches hold a significant place in history as the site of the D-Day landings during World War II. Omaha Beach, Utah Beach, Juno Beach, Gold Beach, and Sword Beach are not only places of natural beauty but also living memorials to the bravery of those who fought for freedom. Visitors can take guided tours to learn about the events of D-Day, visit museums and memorials, or simply reflect on the solemn history of these hallowed shores.

4. Seaside Strolls and Cliffside Views

Beyond the sandy shores, Normandy's beaches offer scenic walking paths and cliffside trails. Visitors can take leisurely strolls along the water's edge, enjoying panoramic views of the coastline. The famous Étretat cliffs provide a dramatic backdrop to the beaches, creating a landscape that has inspired artists for centuries. The combination of sea air and breathtaking vistas makes these walks an essential part of the Normandy beach experience.

5. Culinary Adventures by the Sea

The coastal towns of Normandy are renowned for their seafood, and the beaches offer a perfect setting to savor these maritime delights. Visitors can indulge in freshly caught fish, succulent oysters, and creamy moules marinières at beachside cafés and restaurants. Whether it's a casual

picnic on the sand or a gourmet seafood feast with a view, Normandy's beaches provide the ideal ambiance for a culinary journey by the sea.

6. Family-Friendly Fun in the Sun

Normandy's beaches are a haven for families, offering a range of activities for all ages. Children can build sandcastles, play beach volleyball, or explore tide pools teeming with marine life. Many beaches have designated family areas with lifeguards, making them safe and enjoyable for young swimmers. Family-friendly festivals and events are also held along the coast, providing entertainment for everyone.

7. Seaside Towns and Beach Markets

The charm of Normandy extends beyond its beaches to the quaint seaside towns that dot the coastline. Coastal markets offer a delightful array of local produce, artisan crafts, and souvenirs. Exploring these markets provides a unique opportunity to immerse oneself in the local culture and discover the flavors and craftsmanship of Normandy.

8. Birdwatching and Wildlife Sanctuaries

Nature enthusiasts will find the beaches of Normandy rich in biodiversity. Birdwatchers can spot a variety of seabirds along the shore, including gulls, terns, and sandpipers. Several wildlife reserves and sanctuaries are located near the beaches, providing a chance to observe local flora and fauna in their natural habitat. These serene environments offer a peaceful contrast to the lively beach activities.

9. Romantic Sunset Escapes

As the day draws to a close, Normandy's beaches transform into romantic settings bathed in the warm hues of the setting sun. Couples can take leisurely evening strolls, enjoy beachfront dinners, or simply sit hand in hand while watching the sun dip below the horizon. The tranquil beauty of Normandy's beaches makes them an enchanting destination for couples seeking a romantic getaway.

10. Practical Tips for Beachgoers

Before embarking on a beach adventure in Normandy, it's essential to be prepared. Here are some practical tips for beachgoers:

Check local tide schedules to ensure a safe and enjoyable beach experience.

Pack sunscreen, hats, and sunglasses to protect against the sun's rays.

Respect local wildlife and adhere to any conservation guidelines.

Familiarize yourself with beach safety rules, especially if participating in water sports.

Explore a mix of popular and less-known beaches to discover the diverse coastal landscapes.

Conclusion

Normandy's beaches are a multifaceted destination, offering something for every type of traveler. Whether you seek relaxation, adventure, history, or culinary delights, the coastal wonders of Normandy await. As you explore the sun-drenched sands and the historic shores, you'll discover that Normandy is not just a destination; it's an experience that will linger in your memories long after the tide has rolled away.

Cycling Routes in Normandy: Explore the Picturesque Landscape

Cycling through the charming landscapes of Normandy is a delightful experience for both avid cyclists and leisure riders. With its rolling hills, picturesque countryside, and historic sites, Normandy offers a variety of cycling routes for enthusiasts of all levels. Below are some noteworthy cycling routes, complete with addresses and descriptions to guide you on your two-wheeled adventure.

1. *Vélo Francette*

Distance: Approximately 630 km

Start Point: Ouistreham, near Caen

End Point: La Rochelle, on the Atlantic Coast

Description: Vélo Francette is a long-distance cycling route that passes through Normandy, offering a diverse range of landscapes. Starting in Ouistreham, you'll pedal through lush green countryside, charming villages, and along the banks of the Vire and Mayenne rivers. Take in the beauty of medieval towns like Domfront and Laval before reaching the Atlantic Coast in La Rochelle.

2. *Voie Verte*

Distance: Varied sections, totaling over 300 km

Start/End Points: Various entry points; popular starting points include Thury-Harcourt and Conde-sur-Huisne

Description: Voie Verte, meaning "Green Way," is a network of disused railway lines converted into cycling paths. Explore the Suisse Normande region on the Thury-Harcourt section or ride through the Perche region starting in Conde-sur-Huisne. These paths are ideal for families and leisure cyclists, offering a smooth and car-free route through the scenic Norman countryside.

3. Alabaster Coast Route

Distance: Approximately 150 km

Start/End Points: Le Havre to Tancarville Bridge

Description: Discover the stunning Alabaster Coast by cycling along this picturesque route. Starting in Le Havre, known for its modern architecture, ride along the cliffs and through charming seaside towns like Étretat. Enjoy panoramic views of the English Channel and explore the scenic beauty of this coastal route.

4. D-Day Landing Beaches Route

Distance: Varies; recommended sections total around 80 km

Start/End Points: Utah Beach to Pegasus Bridge

Description: For history enthusiasts, the D-Day Landing Beaches Route takes you along the beaches where the Allied forces landed on June 6, 1944. Starting at Utah Beach and ending at Pegasus Bridge, cyclists can explore the historic sites, museums, and memorials dedicated to the events of D-Day.

5. Seine Valley Route

Distance: Approximately 160 km

Start/End Points: Le Havre to Rouen

Description: Follow the winding Seine River through the lush greenery of the Seine Valley. This route takes you from the maritime city of Le Havre to the historic city of Rouen. Enjoy the tranquility of the riverbanks, pass through charming villages, and marvel at the impressive architecture along the way.

Normandy's cycling routes offer a perfect blend of natural beauty, historical significance, and cultural richness. Whether you're a seasoned cyclist or a casual rider, these routes provide a unique perspective of this enchanting region. So, gear up, grab your helmet, and pedal your way through the picturesque landscapes of Normandy. Happy cycling!

Vélo Francette: A Journey Through Time and Terrain

Cycling has long been hailed as an excellent way to explore the diverse landscapes and cultures of a region, and few places offer a more enchanting cycling experience than Normandy, France. One particularly captivating route that beckons cyclists is the Vélo Francette. Stretching approximately 630 kilometers from Ouistreham near Caen to La Rochelle on the Atlantic Coast, Vélo Francette is not just a cycling route; it's a journey through history, picturesque landscapes, and the heart of France.

Beginning our pedal-powered adventure in the quaint town of Ouistreham, the starting point of Vélo Francette, cyclists are greeted by the gentle waves of the English Channel. This coastal town, with its historic significance dating back to the Second World War's D-Day landings, serves as the gateway to an immersive journey through the heart of Normandy.

Leaving Ouistreham, the route meanders through a patchwork of green fields, charming villages, and historic sites. The cyclists pedal through the Vire Valley, a region rich in natural beauty and dotted with picturesque hamlets. This is rural Normandy at its finest — a landscape that seems to have paused in time, where the rhythmic sound of bicycle wheels replaces the hustle and bustle of modern life.

As the journey continues, cyclists find themselves in the medieval town of Domfront. This well-preserved town, perched on a hill overlooking the Varenne River, invites riders to explore its cobblestone streets and discover its medieval architecture. The imposing ruins of Domfront Castle add a touch of historical grandeur to the surroundings, transporting cyclists back to an era of knights and feudal lords.

The route's path follows the meandering course of the Vire River, leading cyclists through the picturesque town of Mortain. Here, the cascading waterfalls of the Grande Cascade offer a refreshing break, a chance to connect with nature amid the rhythm of the ride. The pastoral landscapes of Normandy unfold like a living canvas, with each pedal stroke revealing a new scene of rolling hills, orchards, and charming farmhouses.

A highlight of Vélo Francette Is its passage through Laval, a city that seamlessly blends the medieval with the modern. Cyclists can explore the old town, with its half-timbered houses and narrow alleys, or take a leisurely ride along the Mayenne River, absorbing the tranquility that emanates from its waters.

As the route progresses southward, cyclists approach the Loire Valley, renowned for its vineyards and historic châteaux. This leg of the journey introduces a different kind of beauty — one characterized by vine-covered hills, sprawling estates, and the unmistakable scent of the region's wines.

Reaching the final stretch of Vélo Francette, riders are rewarded with the breathtaking landscapes of Marais Poitevin, also known as "Green Venice." The intricate network of canals, lush marshlands, and quaint villages make this region a fitting conclusion to the journey. The canal-side paths provide a serene cycling experience, a chance to reflect on the miles traveled and the stories witnessed along the way.

The ultimate destination of La Rochelle awaits cyclists with its historic harbor, vibrant waterfront, and a sense of accomplishment that comes from completing a remarkable journey. La Rochelle, with its maritime charm and architectural treasures, serves as a fitting conclusion to the Vélo Francette adventure.

In conclusion, Vélo Francette is more than just a cycling route; it's a journey through the soul of Normandy and beyond. It's a pilgrimage through landscapes that have witnessed centuries of history, where the echoes of the past harmonize with the hum of bicycle wheels. For those seeking an immersive and enriching experience on two wheels, Vélo Francette is an invitation to explore the heart of France and create memories that will last a lifetime.

Exploring Normandy's Picturesque Landscapes on the Voie Verte

Cycling enthusiasts and nature lovers alike find a haven in Normandy, a region blessed with rolling hills, serene countryside, and rich historical heritage. Among the myriad of cycling routes that crisscross this enchanting region, the Voie Verte stands out as a gem, offering riders a unique and immersive experience.

Voie Verte, translated as the "Green Way," is a network of disused railway lines transformed into scenic cycling paths. These paths traverse the heart of Normandy, unveiling its hidden treasures to those who pedal through its landscapes. With a total length of over 300 kilometers, the Voie Verte is a haven for cyclists of all levels, from families seeking a leisurely ride to seasoned cyclists yearning for an immersive journey.

One of the remarkable aspects of the Voie Verte is its accessibility. With various entry points and popular starting locations such as Thury-Harcourt and Conde-sur-Huisne, cyclists can choose a route that suits their preferences and capabilities. This inclusivity has contributed to the Voie Verte's popularity, making it a beloved destination for both locals and visitors seeking an active exploration of Normandy.

The Thury-Harcourt section of the Voie Verte is particularly enchanting. As cyclists pedal through this area, they are treated to the beauty of the Suisse Normande region. This part of Normandy is characterized by its verdant landscapes, meandering rivers, and charming villages. The smooth and well-maintained path ensures a comfortable ride, allowing cyclists to focus on soaking in the natural beauty around them.

Conde-sur-Huisne, another popular starting point for the Voie Verte, takes cyclists on a journey through the Perche region. This area is known for its picturesque countryside, dotted with orchards, meadows, and historic villages. Riding along this section of the Voie Verte is like traveling back in time, as cyclists pass by ancient stone houses and traditional French farms.

Throughout the Voie Verte, cyclists are treated to a kaleidoscope of landscapes. The changing scenery includes dense forests, open fields, and occasional glimpses of charming watermills. The absence of motorized vehicles ensures a peaceful and serene environment, allowing riders to connect with nature and appreciate the tranquility that Normandy has to offer.

As cyclists traverse the Voie Verte, they'll encounter not only natural beauty but also cultural and historical richness. The old railway stations along the route have been repurposed, some serving as rest areas for cyclists and others transformed into local museums or art installations. These remnants of the region's industrial past add a layer of historical significance to the cycling journey.

One of the distinctive features of the Voie Verte is its adaptability to various interests. Families with children can comfortably explore sections of the route suitable for all ages, enjoying a leisurely ride surrounded by nature. Meanwhile, more experienced cyclists can tackle longer stretches, relishing the challenge of a more extended journey through Normandy's diverse landscapes.

The Voie Verte is not just a path for cyclists; it's a gateway to discovering the essence of Normandy. Along the route, cyclists can detour into charming villages, stopping at local markets to sample regional delicacies. This immersion into the local culture is a unique aspect of cycling through Normandy, allowing travelers to forge a deeper connection with the people and traditions of the region.

While the Voie Verte offers a year-round cycling experience, each season brings its own enchantment. Spring blankets the route in a burst of blossoms and fresh greenery, while summer bathes the landscape in warm sunlight. Autumn transforms the path into a mosaic of vibrant colors as leaves change, and winter offers a different charm, with crisp air and a serene atmosphere.

Safety and convenience are paramount on the Voie Verte. Cyclists can find rental services near popular entry points, allowing them to embark on their journey even if they don't have their own bikes. Well-marked signposts guide riders along the path, ensuring that they can navigate the route with ease. The flat and even terrain of the former railway lines makes the Voie Verte accessible to cyclists of varying skill levels.

The Voie Verte is not just a local attraction; it's part of a broader European network of greenways. This interconnection provides ambitious cyclists with the opportunity to extend their journey beyond Normandy, exploring neighboring regions and even other countries. The sense of continuity and exploration that the Voie Verte offers is a testament to the interconnectedness of cycling routes across Europe.

In conclusion, the Voie Verte is more than just a cycling route; it's a gateway to the soul of Normandy. Its meandering paths unveil the region's natural beauty, historical significance, and

cultural richness. Whether you're a casual cyclist seeking a leisurely ride or an avid adventurer yearning for a more challenging journey, the Voie Verte beckons, promising an unforgettable exploration of one of France's most enchanting regions. So, saddle up, pedal away, and let the Voie Verte be your guide through the picturesque landscapes of Normandy.

The Alabaster Coast Route: Cycling along the Stunning Cliffs of Normandy

Stretching along the northern coast of France, the Alabaster Coast in Normandy is a breathtakingly beautiful region renowned for its dramatic cliffs, charming seaside towns, and panoramic views of the English Channel. For cycling enthusiasts, the Alabaster Coast Route offers an unforgettable journey through this picturesque landscape. This cycling adventure takes you from the modern city of Le Havre to the iconic Tancarville Bridge, immersing you in the natural beauty and cultural richness of Normandy.

Le Havre, the starting point of the Alabaster Coast Route, is a city with a unique history and a blend of modern and UNESCO-listed architecture. As you set out on your cycling adventure, take a moment to explore the city's waterfront, where the combination of contemporary design and maritime charm creates a distinctive atmosphere.

From Le Havre, the cycling route leads you along the rugged coastline, offering spectacular views of the cliffs that give the region its name. The cliffs of the Alabaster Coast, made of chalk, rise majestically from the sea, creating a stunning contrast with the deep blue waters below. The sensation of the salty sea breeze on your face and the sound of waves crashing against the cliffs make for a sensory experience that adds to the allure of the journey.

Étretat, a small town nestled between towering cliffs, is a highlight along the route. The famous natural arches and needle-like formations of the cliffs at Étretat have inspired artists for centuries. As you cycle through the town, you'll have the opportunity to pause and admire these natural wonders. The views from the cliff tops are particularly enchanting, offering a panoramic vista of the coastline and the vastness of the English Channel.

Continuing along the Alabaster Coast, you'll encounter other charming seaside towns such as Fécamp and Yport. Fécamp, known for its historic Benedictine Palace, is a town with a rich maritime heritage. The impressive structure of the palace, perched on the hill overlooking the town and the sea, is a testament to Fécamp's historical significance.

Yport, a smaller and more intimate coastal village, provides a contrast to the larger towns along the route. With its narrow streets, traditional architecture, and a sense of tranquility, Yport invites cyclists to explore its charm at a leisurely pace. The small harbor and pebble beach add to the coastal ambiance, making it a perfect spot to take a break and absorb the coastal serenity.

As you pedal along the Alabaster Coast Route, you'll encounter not only natural wonders but also historical sites that add layers to the journey. The Benedictine Abbey in Montivilliers, a short detour from the main route, is a hidden gem. The abbey, dating back to the 7th century, showcases Norman Romanesque architecture and provides a glimpse into the region's medieval history.

The cycling route culminates at the Tancarville Bridge, an impressive suspension bridge that spans the Seine River. The bridge, with its iconic towers and sweeping views of the river, marks the end of the Alabaster Coast Route. The journey concludes with a sense of accomplishment and a collection of memories of the stunning landscapes, charming towns, and cultural treasures encountered along the way.

In conclusion, the Alabaster Coast Route is a cycling adventure that combines natural beauty, cultural exploration, and the joy of outdoor activity. Whether you're an avid cyclist seeking a challenging route or a leisure rider in search of scenic landscapes, this route offers an immersive experience of Normandy's coastal charm. From the vibrant city of Le Havre to the iconic Tancarville Bridge, the Alabaster Coast Route invites you to discover the enchanting world of Normandy from the saddle of your bicycle.

D-Day Landing Beaches Route

The D-Day Landing Beaches Route in Normandy stands as a solemn testament to one of the most pivotal moments in modern history—the Allied invasion of Normandy on June 6, 1944. Commonly known as D-Day, this day marked the beginning of the end for Nazi occupation in Western Europe. The beaches where this audacious landing took place have since become hallowed ground, and the D-Day Landing Beaches Route offers a poignant journey through history.

Stretching along the coastline of Normandy, the route encompasses several key beaches where the Allied forces, primarily American, British, and Canadian troops, landed to liberate Europe from the grip of Nazi Germany. Each beach has its own unique story and significance, and

collectively, they form a mosaic of heroism, sacrifice, and the inexorable march towards freedom.

Utah Beach, situated on the westernmost flank of the invasion, witnessed the landing of the United States 4th Infantry Division. Its sandy shores, once the theater of intense and chaotic battles, now bear witness to the tranquility of the present. The Utah Beach Museum stands as a living testament to the valor of those who fought on these shores. Artifacts, personal accounts, and remnants of the war bring to life the challenges faced by the soldiers on that fateful day.

Omaha Beach, often referred to as "Bloody Omaha," was the site of the bloodiest and most challenging landing on D-Day. The American forces faced fierce German resistance, leading to heavy casualties. The Normandy American Cemetery and Memorial, overlooking the beach, is a poignant reminder of the cost of freedom. Rows upon rows of white crosses and Stars of David pay homage to the soldiers who paid the ultimate sacrifice.

Moving eastward, Gold Beach was assigned to British forces, specifically the 50th (Northumbrian) Infantry Division. The beachhead here played a crucial role in establishing a link between the British and Canadian forces landing at Juno Beach. Today, remnants of the Mulberry Harbor, a temporary harbor constructed to facilitate the rapid offloading of troops and supplies, are still visible just off the coast.

Juno Beach was the responsibility of Canadian forces on D-Day. Despite facing challenging conditions, the Canadians achieved significant success in their objectives. The Juno Beach Centre, a museum and cultural center, provides a comprehensive look at Canada's role in World War II. It not only commemorates the sacrifices made but also educates visitors about the broader historical context of the war.

Sword Beach, the easternmost of the D-Day Landing Beaches, was a key target for British and Free French forces. The British 3rd Infantry Division landed here, and the beach was taken with relatively fewer casualties compared to Omaha and Utah. Pegasus Bridge, a critical objective for securing the eastern flank, was captured in a daring glider assault and remains a symbol of airborne forces' contribution to the success of D-Day.

Beyond the beaches, the D-Day Landing Beaches Route extends inland, allowing travelers to explore the towns, villages, and countryside that played pivotal roles in the D-Day operations. Sainte-Mère-Église, the first town liberated by the Allies, boasts the Airborne Museum, recounting the story of the paratroopers who landed there.

The route also leads to the town of Bayeux, home to the world-famous Bayeux Tapestry. While not directly related to D-Day, the tapestry offers a fascinating historical narrative, depicting the events leading up to the Norman Conquest of England in 1066.

The D-Day Landing Beaches Route is a journey through time, a pilgrimage to the sites where the fate of nations was decided. It's an opportunity to reflect on the courage of those who stormed these beaches under a hail of gunfire and to honor the memory of those who gave their lives for the cause of freedom. The scars of war are still visible on the landscape, serving as a stark reminder of the price paid for the liberties we often take for granted today. Visiting the D-Day Landing Beaches is not just a historical tour; it's an emotional and humbling experience that leaves an indelible mark on the hearts and minds of those who undertake this solemn pilgrimage.

Seine Valley Route

Exploring the Seine Valley on a cycling adventure is a captivating journey through the heart of Normandy. Stretching approximately 160 kilometers from Le Havre to Rouen, this route unveils the region's rich tapestry of landscapes, culture, and history. As you pedal along the Seine River, you'll encounter the tranquil beauty of riverbanks, charming villages, and the remarkable architecture that defines this part of France.

The journey commences in Le Havre, a maritime city with a unique blend of modernity and history. As you set out from the port, the refreshing sea breeze accompanies you along the early stretches of the route. Le Havre's urban landscape, largely reconstructed after World War II, presents a distinct character, with architectural gems such as the Saint Joseph Church, a UNESCO World Heritage site.

Leaving the city behind, the route takes you into the heart of the Seine Valley. The countryside unfolds, revealing lush greenery and a slower pace of life. Cycling along the riverbanks provides a serene experience, with the Seine's waters reflecting the changing colors of the sky.

As you pedal deeper into the Seine Valley, you encounter picturesque villages that seem frozen in time. Quaint houses with flower-filled gardens line the route, and the sound of church bells resonates in the air. Each village has its own story to tell, and the locals, warm and welcoming, add a personal touch to your journey.

One of the notable stops along the Seine Valley Route is the town of Jumièges, known for its impressive abbey ruins. The Jumièges Abbey, with its towering walls and Gothic architecture, stands as a testament to the region's medieval history. Take a break from cycling to explore the abbey grounds, where echoes of the past whisper through the stones.

Continuing on, the route meanders through apple orchards and pastures, showcasing the agricultural richness of Normandy. The region is renowned for its apple-based products,

including the famous Normandy cider and Calvados. Consider stopping at a local orchard or cidery to savor the flavors of the land.

As the Seine Valley Route progresses, the landscape transforms, offering panoramic views of the river and its surrounding hills. Cycling enthusiasts will appreciate the varying terrain, with gentle slopes providing a welcome challenge. The route caters to cyclists of different skill levels, making it accessible for both seasoned riders and those seeking a leisurely cycling experience.

Approaching Rouen, the capital of Normandy, the Seine Valley Route introduces you to the city's majestic skyline. Rouen's historical significance is evident in its architecture, with the iconic Rouen Cathedral and the Gros Horloge (Great Clock) standing as symbols of the city's grandeur. Take time to explore the narrow medieval streets of the Old Town, where timber-framed houses transport you to another era.

Rouen's role in the life of Joan of Arc is commemorated at various sites, including the Joan of Arc Church and the Place du Vieux Marché, where the courageous young woman met her fate. The city's vibrant atmosphere, cultural attractions, and culinary delights offer a fitting conclusion to your cycling odyssey through the Seine Valley.

In conclusion, the Seine Valley Route is a captivating cycling adventure that immerses you in the enchanting landscapes and cultural richness of Normandy. Whether you seek a leisurely ride through charming villages or a more challenging cycling experience, this route caters to diverse preferences. As the Seine River accompanies you on this journey, each pedal stroke unfolds a new chapter of the region's history and natural beauty. So, saddle up, embrace the rhythm of the Seine Valley, and let the enchantment of Normandy unfold before you.

Water Sports

Normandy, with its picturesque coastline along the English Channel, offers a vibrant tapestry of water sports that beckon adventure seekers and nature lovers alike. From the bustling beaches to the serene estuaries, the region provides an array of aquatic activities that cater to diverse interests. In this exploration of water sports in Normandy, we delve into the rich tapestry of experiences awaiting those who venture into its refreshing waters.

Normandy's extensive coastline, spanning over 600 kilometers, sets the stage for an aquatic playground that embraces both thrill-seekers and those seeking a more tranquil escape. The region's diverse topography, featuring cliffs, dunes, and expansive sandy shores, lays the groundwork for an array of water-based adventures.

Surfing enthusiasts find their haven along Normandy's shores, where the Atlantic swells meet the English Channel's currents. From the renowned beaches of Etretat to the less-explored gems like Barneville-Carteret, surfers of all levels can ride the waves, guided by experienced instructors or embarking on solo journeys in search of the perfect break.

Kitesurfing, a thrilling marriage of wind and water, is another hallmark of Normandy's aquatic offerings. The open stretches of beach, particularly in locations such as Courseulles-sur-Mer and Ouistreham, provide the ideal canvas for kitesurfers to harness the region's coastal winds, sending them soaring over the waves in a dance of skill and daring.

For those who prefer a more relaxed pace, kayaking and paddleboarding opportunities abound in Normandy's estuaries and coastal inlets. Exploring the meandering Seine River or navigating the tranquil waters around the Cotentin Peninsula allows water enthusiasts to immerse themselves in the region's natural beauty at a leisurely tempo. Nature reserves and bird sanctuaries along the coast provide a scenic backdrop for these serene waterborne adventures.

Normandy's maritime legacy is not confined to its beaches alone; the Seine River, a vital waterway in the heart of the region, invites exploration by boat. River cruises offer a unique perspective on Normandy's landscapes, unveiling charming villages, historic landmarks, and verdant countryside along the way. The transformative journey along the Seine is a testament to the region's ability to seamlessly blend water-based recreation with cultural immersion.

The allure of fishing finds a haven In Normandy's waters, where both seasoned anglers and casual enthusiasts can cast their lines in pursuit of a variety of fish. From sea fishing along the rugged coastline to freshwater angling in the region's rivers and lakes, Normandy's diverse aquatic environments ensure a bounty of experiences for fishing aficionados.

Normandy's commitment to sustainable tourism is evident in its efforts to preserve and protect its coastal ecosystems. Conservation initiatives and marine sanctuaries contribute to the region's appeal as a destination that balances recreation with environmental stewardship. This commitment ensures that future generations can continue to enjoy the pristine waters and diverse marine life that define Normandy's coastal identity.

As the sun sets over the English Channel, Normandy's beaches come alive with the flicker of bonfires, creating an enchanting atmosphere for beachgoers and night surfers alike. The region's vibrant nightlife extends to its shores, where moonlit walks and beachside gatherings underscore the timeless allure of Normandy's coastal landscapes.

In conclusion, Normandy's water sports offer a dynamic fusion of excitement, tranquility, and cultural immersion. Whether riding the waves along its iconic beaches, navigating the meandering rivers, or casting a line into its rich waters, the region invites visitors to forge a deep connection with its aquatic soul. Normandy's maritime tapestry is not just a canvas for recreation; it is a living testament to the region's enduring love affair with the sea.

CHAPTER 4: CULINARY DELIGHTS

Normandy Cuisine Overview

Normandy, nestled in the north-western corner of France, is not only renowned for its picturesque landscapes and historic landmarks but also for its rich and delectable culinary traditions. The region's cuisine is a celebration of its bountiful agricultural resources, coastal proximity, and a long history of gastronomic excellence. From savory dishes to sweet treats, Normandy's culinary offerings reflect the diversity and vitality of its people.

At the heart of Normandy's culinary identity is its emphasis on fresh, locally sourced ingredients. The region's fertile soil provides an abundance of fruits, vegetables, and grains, while its proximity to the English Channel ensures a steady supply of high-quality seafood. These elements form the foundation of many iconic Normandy dishes.

Normandy is perhaps best known for its dairy products, particularly its world-famous butter and cheeses. The lush pastures of the region are home to contented cows, whose milk is used to create the rich and flavorful Normandy butter. This butter, with its distinct golden hue, imparts a unique taste to a variety of dishes, from simple baguettes to complex sauces.

Cheese enthusiasts will find themselves in paradise in Normandy, as the region produces an array of exceptional cheeses. Camembert, Pont-l'Évêque, and Livarot are just a few of the cheeses that have gained international acclaim. Each cheese tells a story of craftsmanship and tradition, with distinct flavors and textures that reflect the terroir of the region.

Seafood plays a prominent role in Normandy's gastronomy, thanks to its extensive coastline. Oysters harvested from the chilly waters of the English Channel are a delicacy enjoyed throughout the region. Mussels, scallops, and various fish are also featured in local dishes, highlighting the freshness and quality of the seafood available in Normandy.

One cannot delve into Normandy cuisine without mentioning the region's iconic apple orchards. Normandy is renowned for its apples, which are transformed into a myriad of products, including cider, Calvados (apple brandy), and apple-based desserts. The apple orchards, with their neat rows of trees, are not only a sight to behold but also a testament to Normandy's dedication to preserving its culinary heritage.

Normandy's culinary repertoire is further enriched by its traditional dishes, many of which have been passed down through generations. The hearty Norman pot-au-feu, a slow-cooked stew

featuring a medley of meats and vegetables, warms the soul during the colder months. Tripes à la mode de Caen, a dish made with tripe and a rich wine-based sauce, is a testament to the region's commitment to utilizing every part of the animal in its gastronomy.

Sweets lovers will find bliss in Normandy's delectable desserts. Tarte Tatin, a caramelized upside-down apple tart, is a beloved classic that originated in the region. Normandy's apple and pear-based pastries, such as teurgoule and fallue, showcase the versatility of the region's orchard treasures.

Normandy's culinary scene is not just about what's on the plate; it's also about the experience of sharing a meal with loved ones. The region's charming bistros and Michelin-starred restaurants alike offer a warm and inviting atmosphere where locals and visitors come together to savor the flavors of Normandy.

In conclusion, Normandy's cuisine is a tapestry of flavors, textures, and traditions woven together by a deep connection to the land and sea. Whether enjoying a leisurely meal in a quaint village or exploring the bustling markets, one cannot help but be captivated by the culinary magic that defines this region. Normandy's gastronomic heritage is a testament to the notion that food is not just sustenance; it is a reflection of history, culture, and the vibrant spirit of a place.

Exploring Normandy's Local Specialties

Normandy, a region in northern France, is not only renowned for its picturesque landscapes and historical landmarks but also for its rich culinary heritage. The fertile land, abundant seafood, and lush pastures contribute to a diverse and flavorful array of local specialties. In this gastronomic journey, we delve into the unique and delectable foods that define the essence of Normandy.

1. *Camembert Cheese: A Culinary Icon*

No exploration of Normandy's culinary treasures is complete without mentioning Camembert cheese. This creamy and pungent cheese originated in the village of Camembert in the 18th century. Made from cow's milk, Camembert is known for its velvety texture and earthy aroma. Enjoy it on a baguette or as part of a cheese platter, accompanied by a glass of local cider.

2. *Calvados: The Spirit of Normandy*

Calvados, an apple brandy named after the region, is a quintessential Norman drink. Distilled from fermented apple or pear juice, Calvados boasts a robust and fruity flavor. Whether sipped neat or used in cooking to add depth to sauces, this spirit reflects the orchard-covered landscapes of Normandy.

3. *Normandy Cider: A Refreshing Tradition*

Apples are not only destined for Calvados; they also find their way into Normandy's famous apple cider. With a slightly effervescent quality, Normandy cider is a crisp and refreshing beverage that perfectly complements the region's hearty cuisine. Varieties range from sweet to dry, offering options for every palate.

4. Boudin Noir: Black Pudding Excellence

A delicacy that might raise eyebrows but is cherished in Normandy is Boudin Noir, or black pudding. Made from pig's blood, fat, and a mixture of spices, this sausage has a rich, savory flavor. Often enjoyed with apples or mashed potatoes, Boudin Noir showcases the Norman commitment to utilizing every part of the pig in their culinary creations.

5. Seafood Sensations: Oysters and Mussels

Normandy's extensive coastline provides an abundance of seafood, and oysters and mussels take center stage. The briny oysters from the coastal waters are a delicacy best enjoyed fresh with a squeeze of lemon. Mussels, often prepared in a white wine and garlic sauce, reflect the maritime influences on Norman cuisine.

6. Tripes à la Mode de Caen: A Hearty Delight

For those with adventurous tastes, Tripes à la Mode de Caen is a dish that exemplifies Normandy's commitment to using every part of an animal. This traditional dish features tripe (cow's stomach lining) slow-cooked in a savory broth with onions, carrots, and spices. It's a dish that speaks to the region's agricultural roots and resourceful culinary traditions.

7. Normandy Butter: Rich and Creamy

Normandy is renowned for its high-quality dairy, and the butter produced here is no exception. Known for its rich, golden hue and creamy texture, Normandy butter is a staple in the region's cuisine. Whether slathered on a fresh baguette or used in baking, this butter adds a luxurious touch to every dish.

8. Andouille de Vire: Smoky Sausage Delight

Andouille de Vire, a smoky and spiced sausage, is another culinary gem hailing from Normandy. Made with pork tripe and chitterlings, this sausage is seasoned with salt, pepper, and a touch of nutmeg. Often enjoyed grilled or added to stews, Andouille de Vire is a flavorful representation of Norman charcuterie.

9. Normandy Apple Tart: A Sweet Finale

No exploration of Normandy's local specialties is complete without indulging in a slice of Normandy Apple Tart. Made with layers of thinly sliced apples atop a buttery pastry crust, this dessert showcases the region's love affair with apples. Served warm and often accompanied by a dollop of crème fraîche, it's a delightful conclusion to a Norman meal.

Normandy's local specialties tell a story of a region deeply connected to its land and sea. From the creamy richness of Camembert cheese to the smoky allure of Andouille de Vire, each dish reflects the cultural tapestry of this French region. So, as you explore the picturesque landscapes and historic sites of Normandy, be sure to savor the culinary treasures that make this region a feast for the senses.

Exploring Culinary Delights: A Guide to the Best Restaurants and Cafés in Normandy

Welcome to Normandy, where culinary traditions are as rich as the picturesque landscapes. This guide takes you on a gastronomic journey through the region, highlighting some of the best restaurants and cafés that promise an unforgettable dining experience.

1. Le Jardin des Plumes – Giverny

Address: 1 Rue du Milieu, 27620 Giverny, France

Nestled in the charming village of Giverny, Le Jardin des Plumes is a culinary gem that seamlessly blends art and gastronomy. Set in a beautiful garden, the restaurant offers a seasonal menu crafted with locally sourced ingredients. From delicate seafood dishes to decadent desserts, every bite is a celebration of flavor and creativity.

2. La Marine – Port-en-Bessin-Huppain

Address: 6 Quai Félix Faure, 14520 Port-en-Bessin-Huppain, France

For a taste of the sea, head to La Marine in Port-en-Bessin-Huppain. This Michelin-starred restaurant, overlooking the harbor, is renowned for its seafood platters and innovative dishes inspired by the Normandy coast. The chef's meticulous attention to detail ensures a dining experience that reflects both tradition and modernity.

3. Au Vieux Honfleur – Honfleur

Address: 35 Rue Haute, 14600 Honfleur, France

In the heart of Honfleur, Au Vieux Honfleur invites you to savor authentic Norman cuisine in a cozy and historic setting. With its exposed beams and rustic charm, the restaurant exudes warmth. Indulge in classics like Camembert fondue or apple tart while immersing yourself in the ambiance of this quaint eatery.

4. Les Canisses – Le Goulet

Address: 160 Rue Albert Boivin, 27500 Le Goulet, France

For a unique dining experience along the Seine, Les Canisses in Le Goulet offers panoramic views and a menu that celebrates the region's agricultural bounty. From duck confit to locally produced cheeses, each dish is a testament to the chef's commitment to showcasing the flavors of Normandy.

5. Café de Flore – Deauville

Address: 3 Rue Eugène Colas, 14800 Deauville, France

If you're in Deauville and craving a leisurely café experience, look no further than Café de Flore. This iconic establishment, with its Belle Époque décor, is a perfect spot for people-watching while enjoying a cup of coffee and a selection of pastries. It's a haven for those seeking a blend of elegance and relaxation.

Normandy's culinary scene is a fusion of tradition, innovation, and a deep connection to the land and sea. Whether you're indulging in a Michelin-starred feast or sipping coffee in a charming café, each culinary experience in Normandy is a journey into the heart of French gastronomy. Explore these establishments and savor the flavors that make Normandy a haven for food enthusiasts.

Le Jardin des Plumes – Giverny

Nestled in the heart of the picturesque village of Giverny, where Claude Monet once found inspiration for his masterpieces, Le Jardin des Plumes stands as a culinary gem that harmoniously blends art, nature, and gastronomy. As the doors of this enchanting restaurant open, visitors are welcomed into a world where the vibrant colors of the garden find their echo in the culinary creations on the plate.

The address, 1 Rue du Milieu, 27620 Giverny, France, is not just a geographical location but a gateway to an exquisite dining experience. Le Jardin des Plumes is not merely a restaurant; it is an immersive journey into the flavors of Normandy, curated with meticulous attention to detail.

In a region renowned for its impressionist landscapes and floral beauty, Le Jardin des Plumes finds its place as a culinary artist, creating dishes that are a feast for both the eyes and the palate. The restaurant's commitment to sourcing locally is reflected in every aspect of its menu, where each ingredient tells a story of the fertile soils and the bountiful seas that surround Normandy.

The ambiance of Le Jardin des Plumes is an extension of Giverny's artistic heritage. The restaurant is housed in a building that exudes charm, with its rustic architecture and a garden that seems like a canvas painted by Monet himself. As diners step into this haven of gastronomy, they are greeted by an atmosphere that is simultaneously elegant and welcoming.

Le Jardin des Plumes takes pride in its seasonal menu, an ever-changing symphony of flavors that reflects the natural rhythm of the region. The chef's creations are not merely dishes; they

are culinary compositions that showcase the diversity and richness of Normandy's produce. From the freshest seafood to the most succulent meats, each element is carefully selected to create a harmonious ensemble.

The restaurant's commitment to culinary excellence has been recognized with accolades, including a Michelin star, a testament to the dedication of the chefs and the entire team. This recognition is not just a mark of prestige but a promise to diners that every meal at Le Jardin des Plumes is an extraordinary experience.

One of the standout features of the restaurant is its use of local herbs, fruits, and vegetables from the garden itself. The garden, an integral part of the restaurant, is not just a decorative element but a living pantry that inspires the chefs daily. The result is a menu that not only captures the essence of Normandy but also evolves with the changing seasons.

Le Jardin des Plumes offers a degustation experience that allows diners to embark on a culinary journey through the flavors of the region. From the delicate balance of a seafood medley to the robustness of locally sourced cheeses, each course is a chapter in the story of Normandy's culinary heritage.

The wine list at Le Jardin des Plumes is a carefully curated selection that complements the menu. From crisp local whites to bold reds, the wines are chosen to enhance the dining experience, offering a perfect pairing for every dish. The staff, knowledgeable and passionate, is always ready to guide diners through the extensive list, ensuring that every sip enhances the flavors on the plate.

Beyond the exquisite dining rooms, the restaurant offers outdoor seating where guests can enjoy their meals surrounded by the beauty of the garden. In the warmer months, this al fresco option provides a unique experience, allowing diners to savor their meals while immersed in the natural beauty that characterizes Giverny.

Le Jardin des Plumes is not merely a dining destination; it is a cornerstone of Giverny's cultural and gastronomic identity. The restaurant is a testament to the enduring allure of this village, which has captivated artists and travelers for generations. It is a place where the past and present converge, where the spirit of Monet's gardens finds a contemporary expression on the plate.

In conclusion, a visit to Le Jardin des Plumes is not just a meal; it is an exploration of the flavors, artistry, and ambiance that define Giverny and, by extension, Normandy. It is an invitation to savor the essence of the region, where every dish is a brushstroke in the culinary masterpiece that is Le Jardin des Plumes. For those seeking an immersive and unforgettable dining experience, this restaurant in the heart of Giverny is a destination that transcends the ordinary, leaving an indelible impression on all who have the pleasure of dining within its walls.

La Marine - Port-en-Bessin-Huppain

La Marine, nestled in the quaint harbor town of Port-en-Bessin-Huppain, stands as a testament to the culinary excellence that defines Normandy's gastronomic landscape. With a Michelin star adorning its name, this restaurant offers more than just a meal—it's an immersive journey into the flavors of the region, a celebration of seafood, and a showcase of the chef's artistry. Let's delve into the essence of La Marine, exploring its history, ambiance, and, most importantly, its culinary delights.

Port-en-Bessin-Huppain itself is a picturesque fishing village along the coast of Normandy, known for its charming harbor and proximity to the historic D-Day landing beaches. Nestled within this scenic setting, La Marine has become a culinary destination, drawing locals and tourists alike with the promise of an exceptional dining experience.

Upon entering La Marine, guests are welcomed into a world of refined elegance. The décor is a seamless blend of modern sophistication and maritime charm. Soft hues of blue and white echo the colors of the sea, while large windows provide panoramic views of the harbor, creating an ambiance that complements the coastal setting.

The culinary journey at La Marine begins with a menu that reflects a deep connection to the local terroir. The chef, known for his commitment to sourcing the freshest ingredients, crafts a seasonal menu that highlights the bounty of the sea. From the delicate flavors of oysters to the rich, robust taste of freshly caught fish, each dish is a homage to Normandy's maritime heritage.

The attention to detail is apparent in every aspect of the dining experience. From the carefully curated wine list featuring selections that complement the seafood-centric menu to the impeccable service that caters to the needs of each guest, La Marine strives for perfection.

One of the standout features of La Marine is its dedication to sustainability. The restaurant places a strong emphasis on supporting local fishermen and farmers, ensuring that the ingredients used are not only of the highest quality but also ethically sourced. This commitment to sustainable practices adds an extra layer of authenticity to the dining experience, allowing guests to savor their meals with a sense of environmental consciousness.

The tasting menu at La Marine is a culinary voyage that unfolds in multiple acts. Each course is a revelation, showcasing the chef's creativity and mastery of culinary techniques. The menu evolves with the seasons, offering guests a chance to experience the freshest and most vibrant ingredients at their peak.

A signature dish at La Marine might be the seafood platter, a masterpiece of presentation and taste. Laden with the day's catch, it's a visual feast that captures the essence of Normandy's

coastal bounty. The oysters, briny and refreshing, transport diners to the shores from which they were harvested. The langoustines, sweet and succulent, are a testament to the pristine waters of the English Channel.

In addition to the seafood-centric offerings, La Marine takes pride in its exploration of local flavors. Norman cheeses find their way onto the menu, offering a savory interlude before the dessert courses. The apple, a symbol of Normandy's orchard-covered landscapes, takes center stage in innovative desserts that marry tradition with contemporary culinary trends.

The wine pairings at La Marine are a symphony of flavors, carefully curated to enhance the nuances of each dish. From crisp and mineral-rich whites that complement the delicate flavors of seafood to robust reds that stand up to heartier fare, the sommelier's selections are a testament to the meticulous attention given to every aspect of the dining experience.

As the meal concludes, diners are left with a lingering appreciation for the culinary artistry that defines La Marine. The dessert course, perhaps featuring the region's renowned Calvados in a delectable form, is a sweet farewell to a dining experience that transcends the ordinary.

In conclusion, La Marine in Port-en-Bessin-Huppain is not merely a restaurant; it's a culinary institution that embodies the spirit of Normandy. Its Michelin-starred status is a recognition of the commitment to excellence that defines every aspect of the dining experience. From the artfully crafted dishes to the enchanting ambiance, La Marine invites guests to savor the flavors of the sea and the soul of Normandy, making it a must-visit for those seeking an unforgettable gastronomic adventure along the French coast.

Exploring Au Vieux Honfleur: A Culinary Voyage in the Heart of Normandy

Nestled in the heart of the enchanting town of Honfleur, Au Vieux Honfleur stands as a testament to the culinary richness of Normandy. This quaint restaurant, situated at 35 Rue Haute, 14600 Honfleur, France, beckons visitors with its charming façade and promises a gastronomic experience that encapsulates the essence of the region.

As you step into Au Vieux Honfleur, the ambiance transports you to a bygone era. Exposed beams, rustic charm, and a warm, welcoming atmosphere set the stage for a dining experience that goes beyond mere sustenance. It's a journey into the heart of Norman cuisine, where tradition and flavor intertwine.

The menu at Au Vieux Honfleur is a celebration of the local bounty, a homage to the agricultural and maritime treasures that define the culinary identity of Normandy. From the first glance, it becomes evident that each dish is a carefully curated masterpiece, showcasing the chef's dedication to authenticity and quality.

One of the highlights of the menu is the Camembert fondue, a classic Norman dish that encapsulates the rich flavors of the region. The creamy, pungent notes of the Camembert, sourced locally, meld seamlessly with the rustic bread, creating a symphony of taste that lingers on the palate.

As you explore the offerings at Au Vieux Honfleur, you'll encounter a variety of seafood dishes that pay homage to the town's maritime heritage. Meticulously prepared and presented, these dishes provide a sensory journey through the bountiful waters of the English Channel. The freshness of the catch is evident in every bite, reminding diners of the proximity of the sea and the restaurant's commitment to quality.

The apple tart at Au Vieux Honfleur is a sweet revelation. Using locally harvested apples, the chef crafts a dessert that encapsulates the orchard-fresh goodness of Normandy. The delicate balance of sweetness and tartness, combined with a flaky crust, elevates this dessert to a culinary masterpiece.

The wine list at Au Vieux Honfleur is a carefully curated selection that complements the flavors of the dishes. From local ciders to renowned French wines, the beverage menu enhances the dining experience, offering a perfect pairing for every palate.

The staff at Au Vieux Honfleur adds an extra layer of warmth to the dining experience. With a passion for hospitality, they guide patrons through the menu, providing insights into the origin of ingredients and the inspiration behind each dish. It's a personalized touch that makes diners feel not just like customers but cherished guests.

The restaurant's location in Honfleur adds to its allure. Honfleur, with its cobbled streets, historic architecture, and bustling harbor, provides a picturesque backdrop to the culinary delights served at Au Vieux Honfleur. The symbiotic relationship between the town and the restaurant creates a unique atmosphere that is both charming and authentic.

In conclusion, Au Vieux Honfleur is more than a restaurant; it's a culinary voyage that immerses diners in the rich tapestry of Norman flavors. From the first bite of Camembert fondue to the last spoonful of apple tart, every dish tells a story of tradition, quality, and a deep connection to the land. As you dine at Au Vieux Honfleur, you not only savor the flavors of Normandy but also become part of a timeless narrative that celebrates the artistry of French gastronomy.

Les Canisses - Le Goulet

Nestled along the banks of the Seine in the quaint village of Le Goulet, Les Canisses stands as a testament to culinary excellence in the heart of Normandy. This hidden gem offers not just a meal but an immersive experience that marries the breathtaking scenery of the Seine with a menu that celebrates the rich agricultural heritage of the region.

As you approach Les Canisses, the first thing that strikes you is the picturesque setting. The restaurant is strategically situated to provide panoramic views of the Seine, creating an ambiance that effortlessly combines natural beauty with a sense of tranquility. The exterior, adorned with vibrant flowers and lush greenery, invites patrons to a dining experience that is as visually enchanting as it is gastronomically satisfying.

Stepping through the entrance, one is greeted by an atmosphere that seamlessly blends sophistication with warmth. The interior design is a reflection of the rustic charm of Normandy, featuring wooden accents, earthy tones, and large windows that allow natural light to flood the space. The result is an inviting space that feels simultaneously intimate and open, a perfect setting for a memorable dining experience.

The heart and soul of Les Canisses lie in its culinary offerings. The menu is a carefully curated symphony of flavors, drawing inspiration from the bounty of the region. The chef's dedication to showcasing the best of Normandy is evident in every dish, where locally sourced ingredients take center stage. From the first appetizer to the final dessert, each bite tells a story of the land and the sea.

The starters are a tantalizing introduction to the culinary journey that awaits. Diners may find themselves torn between the delicate richness of escargot paired with garlic butter and the freshness of a seafood platter featuring Normandy's famed oysters. The menu caters to a range of palates, offering both familiar classics and innovative creations that showcase the chef's culinary prowess.

As the meal progresses, the main courses further elevate the dining experience. Les Canisses is renowned for its emphasis on seafood, and rightly so. The catch of the day, sourced from local fishermen, is transformed into exquisite dishes that capture the essence of the Seine. Whether it's a perfectly seared fillet of sole or a robust seafood stew, each dish reflects a commitment to quality and a passion for the region's culinary heritage.

However, Les Canisses is not solely a haven for seafood enthusiasts. The menu embraces the diversity of Normandy's agricultural offerings, featuring savory options such as duck confit and hearty dishes that highlight the region's renowned cheeses. The thoughtful balance of flavors and textures ensures that every diner, regardless of their preferences, finds a dish that resonates with their palate.

Accompanying the culinary delights is an extensive wine list that complements the menu with finesse. The sommelier, well-versed in the nuances of both local and international wines, is adept at guiding patrons through the perfect pairing for their chosen dishes. From crisp whites that enhance the freshness of seafood to robust reds that complement heartier fare, the wine selection at Les Canisses is a testament to the restaurant's commitment to a holistic dining experience.

The dessert menu at Les Canisses Is a sweet conclusion to the gastronomic journey. From classic French pastries to innovative creations that incorporate local fruits and flavors, each dessert is a work of art. The presentation is as meticulous as the preparation, with each dish enticing diners to indulge in the final act of this culinary symphony.

Service at Les Canisses is characterized by attentiveness and a genuine passion for hospitality. The staff, well-versed in the intricacies of the menu, is adept at offering recommendations based on individual preferences. The seamless coordination between the kitchen and the front of the house ensures that every aspect of the dining experience is executed with precision, allowing patrons to focus on savoring the moment.

Beyond the delectable food and impeccable service, Les Canisses is a destination that encourages patrons to linger and appreciate the surroundings. The outdoor terrace, overlooking the Seine, is an ideal spot for a leisurely meal on a sunny day or a romantic dinner as the sun sets over the river. The gentle rustling of leaves, the distant sounds of the river, and the ambient lighting create an atmosphere that encourages relaxation and connection.

In conclusion, Les Canisses in Le Goulet is not merely a restaurant; it's an ode to the culinary heritage of Normandy. It's a place where the beauty of the surroundings converges with the skillful artistry of the kitchen to create an experience that transcends a simple meal. Whether you're a seasoned seafood connoisseur, an adventurous food enthusiast, or someone seeking a retreat into the charm of Normandy, Les Canisses welcomes you to a dining experience that lingers in the memory long after the last course is savored.

Café de Flore: A Culinary Haven in Deauville

Deauville, with its timeless elegance and picturesque charm, has long been a magnet for those seeking a respite from the bustling city life. Nestled within this coastal gem is a culinary haven that has stood the test of time—Café de Flore. This iconic establishment, with its Belle Époque décor and rich history, beckons both locals and tourists alike to step into a world where time seems to slow down, and every moment is savored.

Café de Flore, situated at 3 Rue Eugène Colas, 14800 Deauville, France, is more than just a café; it is a cultural institution that has woven itself into the fabric of Deauville's identity. As you approach its entrance, the inviting aroma of freshly brewed coffee and the sound of animated conversations spill onto the charming streets, setting the stage for an unforgettable experience.

The café's façade, adorned with intricate ironwork and classic signage, hints at the nostalgia that awaits within. Stepping through the door is like entering a time capsule, transporting visitors to an era where literary giants, artists, and intellectuals gathered to share ideas and inspiration.

The interior exudes an air of refined simplicity. Dark wood paneling, brass accents, and the gentle hum of patrons engaged in conversation create an ambiance that pays homage to both the café's historical roots and the vibrant energy of contemporary Deauville. Whether you choose to sit at the polished wooden bar, the sidewalk terrace, or in one of the cozy corners, each space has its own unique charm.

Café de Flore's menu is a carefully curated selection of delights that reflects the culinary excellence for which French cafes are renowned. The extensive list of beverages ranges from the finest French wines to expertly crafted cocktails, but it is the coffee that takes center stage. Sourced from premium beans and brewed to perfection, each cup is a testament to the café's dedication to the art of coffee-making.

Pair your beverage of choice with an array of pastries, each more tempting than the last. The selection includes buttery croissants, flaky pain au chocolat, and delicate macarons—a symphony of flavors that elevates the café experience. For those with heartier appetites, the menu extends to include savory delights such as quiches, salads, and artisanal sandwiches, all prepared with the attention to detail that defines Café de Flore.

As you savor the culinary offerings, take a moment to observe the ebb and flow of life around you. The café's clientele is as diverse as its menu, ranging from locals who have made it a daily ritual to visitors eager to immerse themselves in the authentic charm of Deauville. The interplay of languages, the laughter of friends, and the contemplative solitude of solo patrons all contribute to the vibrant tapestry of Café de Flore.

What sets Café de Flore apart is not just its culinary excellence but also its historical significance. Established in 1912, the café quickly became a hub for intellectual and artistic luminaries of the time. Writers such as Jean-Paul Sartre and Simone de Beauvoir found inspiration within these walls, engaging in impassioned discussions that shaped the course of literature and philosophy.

The café's commitment to fostering creativity and dialogue is evident in its continued support of the arts. The walls are adorned with contemporary works of local artists, creating a dynamic gallery that adds a modern touch to the timeless atmosphere. Café de Flore, therefore, is not merely a place to dine; it is a living canvas that reflects the ever-evolving spirit of Deauville.

As the day transitions into evening, Café de Flore undergoes a subtle transformation. The soft glow of ambient lighting, coupled with the rhythm of live music, creates an enchanting ambiance. It is a time when the café transitions from a bustling daytime retreat to an intimate setting where the allure of conversation and connection takes center stage.

The terrace, bathed in the warm glow of streetlights, becomes a coveted spot for those seeking a romantic interlude or a quiet moment of reflection. The gentle sea breeze carries with it the whispers of the nearby ocean, adding a touch of maritime magic to the already enchanting atmosphere.

Café de Flore's role in Deauville's cultural landscape extends beyond its culinary offerings and historic legacy. It is a venue for celebrations, a sanctuary for contemplation, and a canvas for the ever-changing expressions of art and culture. The café's commitment to preserving its heritage while embracing the contemporary ensures that it remains a relevant and beloved fixture in the hearts of those who pass through its doors.

In essence, Café de Flore is a microcosm of Deauville itself—a place where tradition and modernity coexist harmoniously. It is a testament to the enduring allure of this coastal town, where each visit to the café becomes a chapter in a personal narrative, woven into the larger tapestry of Deauville's storied history.

In conclusion, Café de Flore in Deauville is not just a destination for culinary delights; it is an experience that transcends the boundaries of time and culture. As you sip your coffee, indulge in exquisite pastries, and absorb the ambiance, you become part of a legacy that spans generations. In every cup poured and every conversation shared, Café de Flore invites you to be a part of the enduring story that is Deauville.

Normandy Cider and Calvados Tasting

Normandy, a region in northern France renowned for its picturesque landscapes and rich history, is equally celebrated for its unique and flavorful beverages, namely cider and Calvados. These quintessentially Norman libations have deep-rooted traditions that extend back through centuries, creating a cultural tapestry that continues to be woven today.

Cider, the Essence of Normandy

Normandy's orchards are a patchwork of verdant hues, adorned with apple trees that have stood the test of time. Cider-making in Normandy is an art form, passed down through generations. Orchards, often interspersed with charming farms, produce an array of apple varieties, each contributing its distinct flavor profile to the final concoction.

The craft of cider-making begins with the careful selection of apples. From the crisp acidity of the Calville Blanc d'Hiver to the sweet succulence of the Douce Moën, these apples are blended to achieve the perfect balance. Once harvested, the apples are washed, crushed, and pressed to extract the juice. This juice undergoes fermentation, transforming it into the effervescent elixir that is Norman cider.

Normandy's cider comes in various styles, ranging from the slightly sweet to the bone-dry. The effervescence dances on the palate, a testament to the meticulous fermentation process. Locals and visitors alike gather in the region's quaint bistros and rustic cideries to savor this golden nectar, often served in traditional ceramic bowls.

Calvados, Aged Perfection

As the sun sets over Normandy's orchards, another treasure emerges – Calvados, an apple brandy that encapsulates the very essence of the region. Named after the Calvados department, this distilled spirit is a testament to the artistry of Norman distillers.

Calvados production is an intricate process that demands patience and skill. The best apples, often the same varieties used for cider, are handpicked and crushed to extract their juice. This juice is then fermented, creating a base alcohol that serves as the canvas for the masterful strokes of the distiller.

The distilled spirit is aged in oak barrels, a journey that imparts complexity and character. The barrels, often repurposed from other spirits, contribute nuanced flavors to the Calvados. As the years pass, the amber liquid within matures, developing a rich bouquet of aromas that range from the fruity notes of apple to the warmth of the oak.

Calvados is classified based on its age, with designations such as Fine, VSOP (Very Superior Old Pale), and XO (Extra Old). Each sip is a voyage through time, a sensory exploration of the orchards and cellars that birthed this exquisite spirit.

The Tasting Experience

Embarking on a cider and Calvados tasting journey in Normandy is an immersion into the region's soul. Visitors often find themselves in rustic cellars, surrounded by oak barrels and the heady aroma of aging spirits. The tastings are guided by passionate artisans who share not just the beverages but the stories behind each bottle.

Cider tastings are a lively affair. The effervescence tickles the nose as the liquid dances on the tongue. From the subtly sweet "doux" to the bracingly dry "brut," the range of flavors mirrors the diversity of Normandy's apple orchards.

Calvados tastings, on the other hand, are a more contemplative experience. The amber liquid, poured into tulip-shaped glasses, beckons with its aromatic dance. The first sip reveals layers of complexity – the initial burst of apple, the warmth of the alcohol, and the lingering embrace of the oak.

Accompanying the tastings are often local delicacies. Creamy Camembert and pungent Livarot cheeses, crusty baguettes, and buttery Norman pastries provide a perfect complement to the beverages, creating a gastronomic symphony on the palate.

Preserving Tradition in Every Sip

Normandy's cider and Calvados are not just drinks; they are cultural ambassadors, preserving the traditions of the region. The orchards, where gnarled apple trees stand as silent witnesses to centuries gone by, tell a story of resilience and reverence for the land.

As visitors savor the nuanced flavors of Norman beverages, they partake in a ritual that transcends time. The art of cider and Calvados making is a testament to the connection between the people of Normandy and their bountiful land, a connection that is celebrated in every sip, making it not just a tasting but a journey into the heart of this enchanting region.

CHAPTER 5: ACCOMMODATIONS

Normandy Hotels: Where Elegance Meets Comfort

Normandy, known for its picturesque landscapes and rich history, offers a diverse range of accommodations to suit every traveler's taste. Whether you seek a luxurious stay or a cozy retreat, the following hotels promise an unforgettable experience.

1. Château de la Chèvre d'Or

Address: 1 Rue de la Chapelle, 50170 Mont-Saint-Michel, France

Nestled on the enchanting Mont Saint-Michel, this hotel combines medieval charm with modern luxury. Enjoy panoramic views of the bay and experience the tranquility of this historic island.

2. Le Manoir des Impressionnistes

Address: 23 Route de la Corniche, 14600 Honfleur, France

Overlooking the Seine estuary, this elegant manor in Honfleur captures the essence of impressionist art. With beautifully decorated rooms and a garden terrace, it's a haven for art lovers.

3. L'Auberge de l'Aure

Address: 1 Rue Saint-Clair, 14400 Bayeux, France

Situated in the heart of Bayeux, this charming inn offers a blend of historic character and modern comfort. The personalized service and proximity to Bayeux Tapestry make it an ideal choice.

4. Le Grand Hôtel Cabourg – Mgallery

Address: Les Jardins du Casino, 14390 Cabourg, France

With its Belle Époque architecture, this 5-star hotel in Cabourg exudes sophistication. Overlooking the sea, it's a retreat for those seeking luxury and a touch of nostalgia.

5. La Ferme Saint Simeon

Address: 20 Quai Sainte-Catherine, 14600 Honfleur, France

This former cider press turned into a boutique hotel in Honfleur is a haven of peace. Surrounded by gardens, it offers a perfect blend of authenticity and refinement.

6. Hotel de Bourgtheroulde, Autograph Collection

Address: 15 Place de la Pucelle, 76000 Rouen, France

In the heart of Rouen, this 5-star hotel seamlessly combines its medieval heritage with contemporary luxury. The spa, gourmet dining, and opulent rooms make it a top choice.

7. Château La Chenevière

Address: Escures-Commes, 14520 Port-en-Bessin-Huppain, France

Located near the D-Day landing beaches, this 18th-century château offers a tranquil escape. Elegant rooms, a Michelin-starred restaurant, and expansive gardens create an idyllic atmosphere.

8. Le Petit Coq Aux Champs

Address: 9 Route de Rouen, 27520 Bourgtheroulde-Infreville, France

Tucked away in the Norman countryside, this charming hotel provides a rustic yet refined experience. The gourmet restaurant and peaceful surroundings make it a hidden gem.

9. Hotel La Marine

Address: 8 Quai Alexandre III, 14360 Trouville-sur-Mer, France

Overlooking the harbor in Trouville-sur-Mer, this boutique hotel captures the essence of coastal living. Stylish rooms and a seafood-focused restaurant offer a taste of maritime luxury.

10. La Couronne – Hotel Restaurant

Address: 5 Place René Groussard, 50470 La Glacerie, France

Just outside Cherbourg, this historic hotel boasts a Michelin-starred restaurant and cozy rooms. The proximity to both city life and natural beauty makes it a versatile choice.

These addresses provide a starting point for exploring the diverse hotel offerings in Normandy. Each establishment has its unique charm, reflecting the region's rich cultural and historical tapestry. Whether you're drawn to the coastal allure, the medieval ambiance, or the countryside serenity, Normandy's hotels are sure to leave a lasting impression.

Château de la Chèvre d'Or:

Nestled on the iconic Mont Saint-Michel, a marvel of medieval architecture rising dramatically from the sea, the Château de la Chèvre d'Or stands as a testament to timeless elegance and luxurious hospitality. This historic hotel, perched on the rocky island, offers an enchanting retreat where the past and present seamlessly intertwine.

As one approaches the château, the awe-inspiring silhouette against the backdrop of the bay captures the imagination. Mont Saint-Michel, a UNESCO World Heritage site, is renowned for its medieval abbey, narrow winding streets, and commanding views of the surrounding tidal flats. The château, with its charming turrets and stone façade, complements the architectural wonders of the island, adding a touch of sophistication to this ancient marvel.

Stepping through the entrance, guests are transported to a world where time seems to slow down, and every detail is a nod to luxury and refinement. The interior of Château de la Chèvre d'Or is a blend of classic elegance and modern comfort. The lobby, adorned with antique furniture and soft lighting, exudes a warm and welcoming atmosphere. Guests are greeted by a courteous staff, eager to ensure a seamless and memorable stay.

Accommodations at the Château are nothing short of spectacular. The rooms and suites, each uniquely designed, offer panoramic views of the surrounding landscape. Whether overlooking the cobblestone streets of Mont Saint-Michel or the vastness of the bay, every window frames a picturesque scene. The décor is a harmonious blend of period furnishings, plush fabrics, and modern amenities, creating an atmosphere of understated luxury.

One of the highlights of Château de la Chèvre d'Or is its gourmet dining experience. The on-site restaurant, with its Michelin-starred status, takes guests on a culinary journey that mirrors the richness of the surrounding landscape. Fresh seafood, locally sourced produce, and expertly crafted dishes showcase the best of Norman cuisine. Dining here is not just a meal; it's a celebration of flavors, a symphony of taste that lingers in the memory.

The château's terrace provides a breathtaking setting for outdoor dining. As the sun sets over the bay, casting a warm glow on the abbey, guests can savor a glass of fine wine and indulge in the gastronomic delights while immersed in the tranquility of the surroundings.

Beyond the luxurious accommodations and fine dining, Château de la Chèvre d'Or offers a range of amenities to cater to the diverse needs of its guests. The spa, nestled within the château's walls, provides a sanctuary of relaxation. The wellness treatments draw inspiration from the sea and local traditions, creating a holistic experience that rejuvenates both body and soul.

For those seeking a unique venue for weddings or special events, the château's event spaces, with their historic charm and modern facilities, provide an enchanting backdrop. Whether it's an intimate celebration or a grand affair, Château de la Chèvre d'Or ensures that every moment is infused with the magic of Mont Saint-Michel.

As night falls, the château takes on a magical aura. The abbey, illuminated against the dark sky, creates a mesmerizing spectacle. Guests can stroll through the narrow streets of Mont Saint-Michel, now bathed in the soft glow of street lamps, creating a romantic ambiance that transports them to another era.

In the morning, waking up in the embrace of Château de la Chèvre d'Or is a surreal experience. The distant sound of the sea, the timeless architecture outside the window, and the promise of another day in this historic haven make every moment memorable.

Château de la Chèvre d'Or is not just a hotel; it's a destination within a destination. It invites travelers to immerse themselves in the rich history of Mont Saint-Michel while enjoying the pinnacle of luxury. Whether seeking a romantic getaway, a cultural exploration, or simply a retreat from the ordinary, this château stands as a beacon of hospitality, inviting guests to write their own chapter in the story of Mont Saint-Michel.

Le Manoir des Impressionnistes

Le Manoir des Impressionnistes is a captivating hotel located at 23 Route de la Corniche, 14600 Honfleur, France. Situated in the heart of Honfleur, a town renowned for its picturesque beauty and historical significance, Le Manoir des Impressionnistes is more than just a place to stay; it is an experience that seamlessly combines elegance with comfort.

This charming manor stands as a testament to the region's cultural richness. As you approach Le Manoir, you are greeted by its architectural splendor – a graceful blend of traditional Norman style with a touch of contemporary sophistication. The exterior, adorned with climbing ivy and surrounded by manicured gardens, sets the stage for the tranquil atmosphere that awaits within.

The interiors of Le Manoir des Impressionnistes are a harmonious fusion of classic charm and modern luxury. The décor pays homage to the impressionist art movement, with each room thoughtfully designed to reflect the essence of this influential period. Artistic nuances permeate the space, from the choice of color palettes to the carefully curated artwork that adorns the walls.

Accommodations at Le Manoir are a retreat into refined comfort. The rooms and suites, exquisitely furnished, provide a sanctuary for guests seeking relaxation and tranquility. Whether you choose a room with a view of the Seine estuary or one overlooking the well-manicured gardens, every space is designed to evoke a sense of calm and sophistication.

One of the highlights of Le Manoir des Impressionnistes is its commitment to personalized service. The staff, attentive and courteous, goes above and beyond to ensure that guests have a memorable and enjoyable stay. Whether it's assisting with travel arrangements, recommending local attractions, or fulfilling specific requests, the team at Le Manoir prides itself on delivering an exceptional level of hospitality.

The culinary experiencee at Le Manoir is nothing short of extraordinary. The on-site restaurant, with its inviting ambiance and gourmet offerings, beckons guests to indulge in the finest culinary delights. The menu showcases a fusion of traditional Norman flavors and international influences, prepared with the freshest local ingredients. Dining at Le Manoir is a sensory journey that reflects the gastronomic richness of the region.

In addition to its elegant accommodations and exquisite dining options, Le Manoir des Impressionnistes offers a range of amenities to enhance the overall guest experience. The meticulously landscaped gardens provide a serene setting for leisurely strolls or moments of quiet contemplation. The terrace, with its panoramic views of the Seine estuary, is an ideal spot for enjoying a leisurely breakfast or a glass of wine as the sun sets.

For those seeking relaxation, the spa at Le Manoir offers a haven of tranquility. Indulge in a range of rejuvenating treatments, from massages to facials, designed to soothe the mind and invigorate the body. The spa's serene ambiance and skilled therapists create an oasis of well-being, inviting guests to unwind and escape from the stresses of everyday life.

Le Manoir des Impressionnistes is not just a place to stay; it is a venue for special occasions and events. The manor's elegant event spaces, whether it's a wedding, a corporate retreat, or a private celebration, provide a backdrop of timeless beauty. The attentive staff works closely with event organizers to ensure that every detail is meticulously executed, creating memorable moments for guests and hosts alike.

Beyond the confines of the manor, Honfleur beckons with its charm and allure. Le Manoir's strategic location allows guests easy access to the town's historic landmarks, vibrant markets, and quaint streets lined with boutiques and art galleries. Strolling along the cobbled streets, you can immerse yourself in the same landscapes that inspired the likes of Monet and other impressionist painters.

In conclusion, Le Manoir des Impressionnistes is a gem in the heart of Honfleur, offering an experience that transcends the ordinary. From its architectural splendor to its artistic interiors, from its culinary delights to its commitment to personalized service, every aspect of Le Manoir reflects the spirit of the impressionist movement. It is a haven where guests can escape, unwind, and immerse themselves in the timeless beauty of Normandy.

L'Auberge de l'Aure

L'Auberge de l'Aure stands as a testament to the rich tapestry of history and hospitality In the heart of Bayeux, Normandy. Nestled on 1 Rue Saint-Clair, this charming inn invites travelers into a world where tradition meets modern comfort. With its warm ambiance and proximity to Bayeux Tapestry, L'Auberge de l'Aure offers not just a place to rest, but an immersive experience in the cultural richness of the region.

Upon arriving at L'Auberge de l'Aure, visitors are greeted by the quaint exterior that echoes the architectural charm of Bayeux. The stone façade, adorned with blooming flowers, sets the tone for the cozy retreat that awaits within. The inn seamlessly integrates its historic character with contemporary amenities, creating a welcoming atmosphere for guests seeking a blend of old-world charm and modern convenience.

Inside, the reception area exudes a sense of warmth, with friendly staff ready to assist guests with a smile. The décor pays homage to the local culture, with touches of Norman influence evident in the choice of furnishings and artwork. The reception area serves as a gateway to the heart of L'Auberge de l'Aure, where each room tells a story of comfort and style.

The accommodations at L'Auberge de l'Aure are a harmonious blend of classic and contemporary design. The rooms, adorned with tasteful décor, offer a serene retreat for weary travelers. The color palette reflects the soothing tones of the surrounding landscapes, creating an ambiance that encourages relaxation. From cozy single rooms to spacious suites, each space is thoughtfully designed to cater to the diverse needs of guests.

The attention to detail In the rooms is evident in the choice of furnishings, with a focus on comfort without compromising on aesthetics. Soft linens, plush pillows, and carefully selected artwork contribute to the overall ambiance of tranquility. The integration of modern amenities, including high-speed internet and state-of-the-art entertainment systems, ensures that guests experience the comforts of contemporary living.

One of the highlights of L'Auberge de l'Aure is its commitment to providing a personalized experience. The staff, known for their hospitality, goes above and beyond to make guests feel at home. Whether it's offering recommendations for exploring Bayeux or arranging special requests, the team at L'Auberge de l'Aure understands the art of hospitality.

The culinary experience at L'Auberge de l'Aure is a journey through Normandy's gastronomic delights. The on-site restaurant, a culinary gem in its own right, showcases the region's bounty with a menu that reflects the seasonality of local produce. Guests are treated to a gastronomic adventure that highlights the flavors of Normandy, from savory classics to innovative culinary creations.

The dining area itself is an extension of the inn's inviting atmosphere. The ambiance is one of understated elegance, with a combination of ambient lighting and tasteful décor setting the stage for a memorable dining experience. Whether indulging in a leisurely breakfast or savoring a gourmet dinner, guests at L'Auberge de l'Aure are treated to a feast for the senses.

Beyond the confines of the inn, L'Auberge de l'Aure benefits from its strategic location in the heart of Bayeux. The proximity to Bayeux Tapestry, a UNESCO World Heritage Site, is a significant draw for history enthusiasts. Guests can easily immerse themselves in the medieval tale depicted on the tapestry, gaining insights into the events that shaped the region.

Bayeux itself is a charming town with cobbled streets, historic architecture, and a vibrant atmosphere. L'Auberge de l'Aure serves as a convenient base for exploring the local attractions, including the Bayeux Cathedral and the Museum of the Battle of Normandy. The inn's central location allows guests to stroll through the town's cultural and culinary offerings at their leisure.

As evening falls, L'Auberge de l'Aure transforms into a haven of tranquility. The courtyard, adorned with twinkling lights, becomes an enchanting space for guests to unwind. Whether sipping a glass of local wine under the starlit sky or enjoying the quietude of the surroundings, the inn embraces the peaceful rhythm of Bayeux.

L'Auberge de l'Aure's commitment to sustainability adds another layer to its appeal. The inn is mindful of its environmental impact, implementing eco-friendly practices without compromising on the quality of service. From energy-efficient lighting to waste reduction initiatives, L'Auberge de l'Aure strives to be a responsible steward of both its heritage and the planet.

In conclusion, L'Auberge de l'Aure emerges as more than just a place to stay; it is an experience that captures the essence of Bayeux and Normandy. Through its charming accommodations, delectable cuisine, and a commitment to hospitality, the inn invites travelers to immerse themselves in the cultural richness of the region. As guests depart from L'Auberge de l'Aure, they carry not just memories of a comfortable stay but a deep appreciation for the timeless charm of Bayeux.

Le Grand Hôtel Cabourg – Mgallery: A Symphony of Elegance and Coastal Splendor

Nestled in the heart of Cabourg, on the enchanting coast of Normandy, Le Grand Hôtel Cabourg stands as a testament to timeless elegance and seaside luxury. This distinguished 5-star hotel, part of the MGallery collection, weaves together the rich tapestry of history with the modernity of upscale hospitality. With its Belle Époque architecture, panoramic views of the sea, and a commitment to providing a truly immersive experience, Le Grand Hôtel Cabourg captivates visitors from around the world.

As you approach the hotel, the grandeur of its exterior immediately commands attention. The graceful façade, adorned with wrought-iron balconies and ornate detailing, transports guests to a bygone era of glamour and sophistication. The hotel's location, Les Jardins du Casino, adds an extra layer of allure, providing a front-row seat to the mesmerizing beauty of the Normandy coastline.

Upon entering the lobby, guests are greeted by an ambiance that seamlessly blends classic charm with contemporary comfort. The interior design pays homage to the Belle Époque era, with opulent furnishings, crystal chandeliers, and a color palette that reflects the hues of the surrounding sea. The atmosphere is one of refined luxury, setting the stage for an unforgettable stay.

Le Grand Hôtel Cabourg boasts a range of accommodation options, each meticulously designed to cater to the discerning tastes of its guests. From well-appointed rooms to spacious suites, every detail has been considered to ensure a harmonious blend of comfort and style. The sea-facing rooms, in particular, offer breathtaking views of the English Channel, allowing guests to wake up to the soothing sound of waves and the sight of the horizon stretching to infinity.

Dining at Le Grand Hôtel Cabourg is an experience that transcends mere sustenance. The hotel's gastronomic offerings are a celebration of Normandy's culinary heritage, expertly crafted to tantalize the taste buds of even the most discerning connoisseurs. The Michelin-starred restaurant showcases the region's finest produce, offering a symphony of flavors that highlight the freshness and quality of local ingredients.

For those seeking relaxation, the hotel's spa provides a sanctuary of serenity and rejuvenation. From therapeutic massages to indulgent beauty treatments, the spa is designed to transport guests into a state of blissful tranquility. The wellness facilities, including a heated indoor pool and a fitness center, complement the overall commitment to holistic well-being.

Le Grand Hôtel Cabourg is not merely a place to stay; it's a venue for creating memories. The hotel's event spaces, including grand ballrooms and intimate salons, provide an exquisite backdrop for weddings, conferences, and other special occasions. The attentive and professional staff work tirelessly to ensure that every event is executed with precision and a touch of the hotel's signature charm.

Beyond the confines of the hotel, Cabourg beckons visitors to explore its charms. The beach, just steps away, invites leisurely strolls or moments of quiet contemplation by the water's edge. The town itself, with its vibrant promenade, charming shops, and historic landmarks, provides a perfect setting for discovering the unique character of Normandy's coastal life.

In conclusion, Le Grand Hôtel Cabourg – Mgallery is a gem on the Normandy coast, where the elegance of a bygone era meets the comforts of modern luxury. From the moment guests arrive, they are enveloped in an atmosphere of sophistication and grace. This iconic hotel serves not only as a place to rest but as a destination in itself, inviting guests to immerse themselves in the beauty of Cabourg and the timeless allure of Normandy's coastline.

La Ferme Saint Simeon: A Tranquil Haven in Honfleur

Nestled on the shores of the picturesque port town of Honfleur, La Ferme Saint Simeon stands as a testament to timeless elegance and authentic Norman charm. This boutique hotel, housed in a converted cider press, seamlessly blends history, art, and modern luxury to create a haven for those seeking respite from the hustle and bustle of daily life.

The origins of La Ferme Saint Simeon date back to the 17th century when the building served as a traditional Norman farm. Over the centuries, it underwent several transformations, eventually finding its current incarnation as a boutique hotel. Today, the hotel is renowned for its unique ambiance, stunning gardens, and a commitment to providing guests with an unparalleled experience.

One of the defining features of La Ferme Saint Simeon is its commitment to preserving the authenticity of the Norman countryside. The architecture, with its half-timbered façade and rustic charm, reflects the region's traditional style. The careful restoration of the cider press and surrounding buildings showcases a dedication to maintaining the historical integrity of this cultural landmark.

As guests enter the property, they are greeted by meticulously landscaped gardens that exude tranquility. The well-manicured lawns, vibrant flower beds, and the gentle trickle of fountains create a sense of serenity that permeates the entire estate. The gardens not only provide a visual feast but also serve as a retreat where guests can unwind and connect with nature.

Accommodations at La Ferme Saint Simeon are a harmonious blend of comfort and sophistication. The rooms and suites, adorned with tasteful décor and equipped with modern amenities, offer a peaceful retreat. Many of the rooms boast stunning views of the Seine estuary, providing a visual spectacle that complements the overall sense of relaxation.

Dining at La Ferme Saint Simeon is a culinary journey that celebrates the rich flavors of Normandy. The hotel's restaurant, with its Michelin-starred status, showcases a commitment to excellence in both service and gastronomy. Local ingredients, including fresh seafood, artisanal cheeses, and the region's renowned apples, are transformed into culinary masterpieces that pay homage to Normandy's culinary heritage.

The spa at La Ferme Saint Simeon is a sanctuary of well-being, inviting guests to indulge in a range of treatments inspired by both traditional and contemporary practices. The soothing ambiance and skilled therapists create an oasis for relaxation, allowing guests to rejuvenate their mind, body, and spirit.

Beyond the confines of the hotel, Honfleur beckons with its cobbled streets, charming harbor, and vibrant arts scene. La Ferme Saint Simeon's proximity to the town's attractions makes it an ideal base for exploration. Guests can stroll along the Quai Sainte-Catherine, visit art galleries showcasing local talent, or simply savor the maritime atmosphere that has inspired generations of artists.

La Ferme Saint Simeon also caters to events and special occasions, offering a unique venue for weddings, corporate retreats, and private gatherings. The combination of historic charm, exquisite gardens, and impeccable service makes it a sought-after destination for those seeking an unforgettable backdrop for their celebrations.

In conclusion, La Ferme Saint Simeon encapsulates the essence of Normandy's allure. It is more than a hotel; it is a destination that invites guests to immerse themselves in the rich tapestry of the region. Whether savoring gourmet delights, relaxing in the spa, or exploring the surrounding landscapes, visitors to La Ferme Saint Simeon are treated to an experience that transcends the ordinary, making it a cherished gem on the shores of Honfleur.

Hotel de Bourgtheroulde, Autograph Collection

Hotel de Bourgtheroulde, Autograph Collection, stands as a paragon of luxury and sophistication in the heart of Rouen, France. This 5-star establishment, part of the esteemed Autograph Collection by Marriott, seamlessly weaves together the city's medieval heritage with contemporary elegance. As you step into the grandeur of Hotel de Bourgtheroulde, you are greeted by a world where history meets modernity, creating an opulent experience that transcends time.

The hotel occupies a central location at 15 Place de la Pucelle, 76000 Rouen, placing guests in close proximity to the city's cultural, historical, and artistic treasures. The magnificent façade of the building, with its intricate architectural details, sets the tone for the luxurious experience that awaits within.

Entering the lobby, guests are immediately enveloped in an atmosphere of refined luxury. The interior design seamlessly blends classic elements with modern aesthetics, creating a space that is both timeless and contemporary. The lobby serves as a prelude to the sumptuous accommodations and world-class amenities that define Hotel de Bourgtheroulde.

Accommodations at Hotel de Bourgtheroulde are a celebration of comfort and style. The rooms and suites are exquisitely appointed, featuring a harmonious blend of classic furnishings, modern conveniences, and thoughtful details. Each room is a sanctuary of relaxation, offering a respite from the bustling energy of Rouen.

For those seeking the pinnacle of luxury, the hotel's suites provide an unparalleled experience. Spacious and elegantly furnished, these suites boast stunning views of the city and offer a heightened level of privacy and indulgence. Whether staying in a standard room or a lavish suite, guests at Hotel de Bourgtheroulde are treated to an atmosphere of refined comfort.

Dining at the hotel is a gastronomic journey that reflects the culinary excellence for which France is renowned. The on-site restaurants showcase the talents of skilled chefs who curate menus that celebrate the finest in French and international cuisine. From gourmet breakfasts to sophisticated dinners, every culinary experience at Hotel de Bourgtheroulde is a feast for the senses.

The Atrium Restaurant, with its glass roof and elegant décor, provides a charming setting for meals. Guests can savor a range of delectable dishes crafted with precision and creativity. Additionally, the hotel's Le 29 Bar offers a stylish ambiance for enjoying handcrafted cocktails and a curated selection of wines and spirits.

Beyond its accommodations and dining, Hotel de Bourgtheroulde boasts an array of amenities designed to enhance the overall guest experience. The hotel's spa is a haven of relaxation, offering a range of rejuvenating treatments and wellness services. The fitness center provides state-of-the-art equipment for those seeking to maintain their exercise routines while away from home.

One of the standout features of Hotel de Bourgtheroulde is its historic charm. The building itself has a storied past, dating back to the 15th century. Originally a private residence, the structure has witnessed centuries of history, and its preservation and adaptation into a luxury hotel add an extra layer of significance to the guest experience.

Meetings and events at Hotel de Bourgtheroulde are elevated to a level of sophistication and professionalism that befits its status as a luxury establishment. The hotel features versatile event spaces equipped with modern technology and supported by a dedicated events team. Whether hosting a corporate conference, a wedding, or a social gathering, the hotel provides a refined backdrop for memorable occasions.

The location of Hotel de Bourgtheroulde places guests within walking distance of Rouen's iconic attractions. The city itself is a treasure trove of history, with landmarks such as the Rouen Cathedral and the Gros Horloge clock drawing visitors from around the world. Exploring the narrow cobblestone streets and charming squares of Rouen is a delightful journey through the annals of French history.

In conclusion, Hotel de Bourgtheroulde, Autograph Collection, is a jewel in the crown of Rouen's hospitality scene. It seamlessly blends the past with the present, offering guests a luxurious and immersive experience. From its historic façade to its modern amenities, every aspect of the hotel reflects a commitment to excellence and a dedication to providing an unforgettable stay. Whether visiting for business or leisure, Hotel de Bourgtheroulde invites guests to step into a world where luxury knows no bounds.

Château La Chenevière: A Timeless Retreat in Normandy

Nestled amidst the picturesque landscapes of Port-en-Bessin-Huppain in Normandy, Château La Chenevière stands as a testament to the region's rich history and timeless elegance. This 18th-century château, with its ivy-clad walls and manicured gardens, offers a unique blend of luxury, tranquility, and historical charm.

As you approach the château, the grandeur of its architecture becomes immediately apparent. The imposing façade, adorned with classic Norman details, hints at the opulence that lies within. The château's roots trace back to the 1700s when it was originally constructed as a manor house. Over the centuries, it underwent transformations and expansions, ultimately evolving into the splendid residence that guests encounter today.

The Interior of Château La Chenevière reflects a seamless fusion of classic and contemporary design elements. The moment you step through the doors, you are greeted by a sense of refinement that permeates every corner. The reception area, adorned with period furniture and tasteful décor, sets the tone for the sophistication that defines the entire château.

Accommodations at Château La Chenevière are nothing short of luxurious. The guest rooms and suites are individually decorated, each bearing its unique charm and character. High ceilings, antique furnishings, and plush fabrics create an ambiance of understated opulence. Many rooms offer breathtaking views of the surrounding gardens, adding a touch of serenity to the overall experience.

For those seeking the epitome of indulgence, the château's suites provide an exclusive retreat. These spacious abodes feature separate living areas, private balconies, and elegant en-suite bathrooms. The meticulous attention to detail in the design ensures that every guest enjoys a stay characterized by comfort and sophistication.

One of the standout features of Château La Chenevière is its expansive and meticulously landscaped gardens. Spread over several acres, the gardens are a harmonious blend of formal French design and the natural beauty of the Normandy countryside. Wandering through the meticulously manicured pathways, guests encounter hidden alcoves, charming fountains, and blooming flowerbeds. The gardens provide an idyllic setting for leisurely strolls, afternoon tea, or simply unwinding amidst nature's splendor.

The culinary experience at Château La Chenevière is a journey into the heart of Normandy's gastronomic heritage. The on-site restaurant, renowned for its Michelin-starred cuisine, showcases the region's finest produce and culinary traditions. Local ingredients, sourced from nearby markets and artisanal producers, take center stage in a menu that celebrates the flavors of Normandy. Diners can savor exquisite dishes while surrounded by the refined ambiance of the château's dining rooms.

Beyond the culinary delights, Château La Chenevière offers a range of amenities and activities to enhance the guest experience. The outdoor swimming pool, nestled amidst the gardens, provides a refreshing oasis during the warmer months. Additionally, the château boasts tennis courts and a fitness center for those seeking recreational activities.

For special occasions and events, Château La Chenevière provides an enchanting backdrop. The château's elegant event spaces, both indoor and outdoor, cater to weddings, conferences, and other celebrations. The attentive staff works closely with event organizers to ensure that every detail is meticulously planned and executed.

Château La Chenevière's location adds to its allure. Situated near the D-Day landing beaches, the château offers a convenient base for exploring the historic sites and museums that commemorate the events of World War II. Guests can embark on guided tours or choose to explore the surrounding areas at their own pace.

In conclusion, Château La Chenevière stands as a jewel in Normandy's crown, a destination where history, luxury, and natural beauty converge. Whether seeking a romantic getaway, a cultural exploration, or simply a retreat into refined tranquility, this château promises an experience that transcends time. As guests depart through the ivy-covered gates, they carry with them not just memories of a luxurious stay but a sense of having stepped into a bygone era, where the essence of Normandy's charm is captured in the walls of this splendid château.

Le Petit Coq Aux Champs

Le Petit Coq Aux Champs, a hidden gem nestled in the heart of the Norman countryside, stands as a testament to the fusion of rustic charm and refined elegance. This enchanting hotel, located at 9 Route de Rouen, 27520 Bourgtheroulde-Infreville, France, offers a unique retreat for those seeking a tranquil escape.

As you approach Le Petit Coq Aux Champs, the idyllic setting begins to unfold. The hotel is a harmonious blend of traditional Norman architecture and modern amenities. Surrounded by lush greenery and serene landscapes, it exudes a sense of peace and tranquility that immediately transports visitors to a world of relaxation.

The accommodations at Le Petit Coq Aux Champs are a true reflection of the hotel's commitment to providing a memorable experience. The rooms, adorned with tasteful décor and comfortable furnishings, offer a perfect balance of rustic warmth and contemporary luxury. Each space is carefully designed to create a welcoming ambiance, allowing guests to unwind and enjoy the serene atmosphere.

One of the standout features of Le Petit Coq Aux Champs is its gourmet restaurant, where culinary excellence takes center stage. The restaurant, with its intimate and inviting atmosphere, is a haven for food enthusiasts. The menu showcases the finest local ingredients, expertly curated to create dishes that not only satisfy the palate but also celebrate the rich culinary heritage of Normandy.

The culinary experience at Le Petit Coq Aux Champs extends beyond the restaurant. The hotel takes pride in its commitment to sourcing fresh, seasonal produce from local farmers and markets. This dedication to local ingredients is not just a culinary choice but a celebration of the region's agricultural bounty.

The charm of Le Petit Coq Aux Champs extends to its surroundings. The hotel is strategically located to provide easy access to the picturesque landscapes that define the Norman countryside. Guests can explore the rolling hills, meandering rivers, and quaint villages that characterize this enchanting region.

For those seeking a touch of relaxation, the hotel's amenities are designed to cater to every need. Whether enjoying a leisurely afternoon by the tranquil gardens or indulging in a spa treatment, guests at Le Petit Coq Aux Champs are treated to a holistic experience that rejuvenates both the body and the spirit.

Le Petit Coq Aux Champs also caters to events and special occasions, offering a charming venue for weddings, celebrations, and corporate gatherings. The combination of scenic surroundings and impeccable service makes it a sought-after destination for those looking to create lasting memories.

As evening falls, the ambiance at Le Petit Coq Aux Champs takes on a magical quality. The subtle lighting, coupled with the sounds of nature, creates an intimate and romantic atmosphere. It's a perfect setting for a quiet dinner or a celebratory toast under the starlit Norman sky.

The hotel's commitment to excellence is evident in the personalized service provided to each guest. The staff at Le Petit Coq Aux Champs goes above and beyond to ensure that every aspect of a guest's stay exceeds expectations. From arranging bespoke experiences to offering local insights, the team is dedicated to creating a memorable and authentic Norman experience.

Le Petit Coq Aux Champs stands as a testament to the timeless allure of the French countryside. It is a place where the past and the present converge, offering a haven of comfort and sophistication in the midst of nature's beauty. For those seeking a retreat that captures the essence of Norman hospitality, Le Petit Coq Aux Champs is a destination that promises an unforgettable experience.

Hotel La Marine

Hotel La Marine, located at 8 Quai Alexandre III, 14360 Trouville-sur-Mer, France, stands as a testament to the timeless allure of coastal living. Perched on the edge of Trouville-sur-Mer's bustling harbor, this boutique hotel effortlessly blends modern comfort with a touch of maritime charm. As one of the prominent establishments in this picturesque seaside town, Hotel La Marine offers an intimate and inviting retreat for travelers seeking a coastal escape.

The hotel's location on Quai Alexandre III provides guests with a front-row seat to the daily rhythms of a lively fishing port. From the windows of Hotel La Marine, one can witness the ebb and flow of the tides, the comings and goings of fishing boats, and the vibrant activities of the harbor. This proximity to the heart of Trouville-sur-Mer adds a distinctive character to the guest experience, allowing visitors to immerse themselves in the authentic maritime atmosphere.

Upon entering Hotel La Marine, guests are greeted by a warm and welcoming ambiance. The interior design pays homage to the nautical heritage of the region, with subtle maritime touches that create a sense of cohesion with the surrounding environment. The lobby, adorned with marine-themed décor, sets the tone for the overall aesthetic of the hotel, where classic elegance meets coastal comfort.

Accommodations at Hotel La Marine are designed to provide a haven of relaxation for guests. The rooms are thoughtfully decorated, featuring a harmonious blend of soothing colors and contemporary furnishings. Many rooms offer breathtaking views of the harbor or the charming streets of Trouville-sur-Mer, allowing guests to wake up to the sight and sounds of this enchanting coastal town.

The hotel's commitment to guest comfort is further exemplified by its range of amenities. Each room is equipped with modern conveniences, ensuring a pleasant stay for both leisure and

business travelers. High-quality linens, well-appointed bathrooms, and complimentary toiletries contribute to the overall sense of luxury that Hotel La Marine strives to provide.

For culinary enthusiasts, Hotel La Marine boasts a restaurant that is as much a destination for locals as it is for guests. The restaurant's menu showcases the region's bountiful seafood offerings, with an emphasis on fresh, locally sourced ingredients. The skilled chefs at Hotel La Marine craft dishes that celebrate the rich maritime heritage of Trouville-sur-Mer, offering a gastronomic journey through Normandy's coastal flavors.

The dining experience at Hotel La Marine extends beyond the plate, as the restaurant's ambiance is carefully curated to enhance the overall enjoyment of each meal. Large windows allow natural light to flood the dining area during the day, creating a bright and airy space. In the evening, the soft glow of ambient lighting adds a touch of intimacy, making it an ideal setting for a romantic dinner or a celebratory meal with friends and family.

In addition to its gastronomic offerings, Hotel La Marine provides a range of services and facilities to enhance the guest experience. A well-appointed bar invites patrons to unwind with a carefully crafted cocktail or a selection from the impressive wine list. The hotel also features event spaces that are suitable for both intimate gatherings and business meetings, with the added benefit of panoramic views of the harbor.

Beyond the confines of the hotel, guests are invited to explore Trouville-sur-Mer and its surroundings. The hotel's central location makes it convenient for visitors to stroll along the waterfront promenade, visit local markets, or indulge in a leisurely afternoon at the nearby sandy beaches. For those with an adventurous spirit, the hotel can assist in organizing excursions and activities, allowing guests to make the most of their time in this charming coastal town.

As a hub of maritime activity, Trouville-sur-Mer has its own unique charm that complements the more well-known destinations in Normandy. While neighboring Deauville may be celebrated for its glamorous atmosphere, Trouville-sur-Mer captures the essence of a traditional fishing port with its colorful boats, seafood markets, and lively waterfront ambiance. Hotel La Marine, situated at the heart of this maritime haven, provides an ideal vantage point for visitors to savor the authentic coastal experience.

In conclusion, Hotel La Marine emerges as a gem on the shores of Trouville-sur-Mer, offering a delightful blend of comfort, elegance, and maritime charm. The hotel's commitment to providing a memorable experience is evident in its meticulous attention to detail, from the thoughtfully designed rooms to the delectable offerings at its restaurant. For travelers seeking a coastal retreat that immerses them in the authentic spirit of Normandy, Hotel La Marine stands as a beacon of hospitality on the shores of Trouville-sur-Mer.

La Couronne – Hotel Restaurant

La Couronne – Hotel Restaurant, located at 5 Place René Groussard, 50470 La Glacerie, France, is a historic establishment that embodies the essence of French hospitality and culinary excellence. This timeless hotel and restaurant, just outside Cherbourg in Normandy, seamlessly blends tradition with modern comforts, offering guests a unique and memorable experience.

Nestled in the charming town of La Glacerie, La Couronne has stood the test of time, becoming a cherished landmark with a rich history dating back to its inception. The hotel exudes an old-world charm, evident in its architecture, décor, and the warmth of its hospitality. Renowned for its Michelin-starred restaurant, La Couronne is a culinary haven that attracts discerning diners and travelers seeking a gastronomic adventure.

The hotel's façade, adorned with classic Norman architecture, sets the tone for the experience that awaits guests. As you approach, the welcoming ambiance of La Couronne becomes palpable, inviting you to step into a world where every detail has been carefully considered. The exterior, with its charming windows and flower-filled window boxes, hints at the refined interior that awaits within.

Upon entering La Couronne, guests are greeted by an atmosphere that seamlessly marries the historic charm of the building with contemporary luxury. The lobby, adorned with antique furniture and tasteful décor, serves as a prelude to the elegance that defines the entire establishment. The reception area, manned by a courteous and attentive staff, sets the tone for the personalized service that guests can expect throughout their stay.

Accommodations at La Couronne are a testament to the hotel's commitment to providing a comfortable and luxurious retreat. The rooms, each uniquely decorated with a blend of classic and modern elements, offer a haven of tranquility. From cozy single rooms to spacious suites, every corner exudes a sense of refinement, with attention to detail evident in the choice of furnishings, color schemes, and amenities.

The Michelin-starred restaurant at La Couronne stands as a culinary gem, drawing both locals and travelers alike. With a focus on seasonal and locally sourced ingredients, the restaurant's menu is a celebration of Normandy's rich gastronomic heritage. The talented chefs curate dishes that showcase the region's bounty, offering a symphony of flavors that captivate the palate.

The dining experience at La Couronne is not just about the exceptional cuisine; it's a journey through the artistry of French culinary traditions. The restaurant's ambiance, with its soft lighting, carefully arranged tables, and attentive staff, elevates every meal into a memorable

occasion. Whether savoring a leisurely breakfast, indulging in a gourmet lunch, or experiencing an intimate dinner, guests are treated to a culinary voyage that reflects the hotel's commitment to excellence.

The wine cellar at La Couronne is a testament to the establishment's dedication to providing a comprehensive and curated dining experience. Featuring an extensive selection of wines, including local vintages and international favorites, the cellar complements the menu with expertly chosen pairings. The sommeliers at La Couronne are well-versed in the art of wine selection, enhancing the overall dining experience.

In addition to its culinary offerings, La Couronne provides a range of facilities and services to ensure a comfortable and memorable stay. The hotel's event spaces are well-suited for weddings, conferences, and special occasions, with a dedicated team available to assist in planning and execution. The grounds, with manicured gardens and outdoor seating areas, offer a serene environment for relaxation and reflection.

For those seeking a balance between exploration and relaxation, La Couronne's location proves advantageous. Situated just outside Cherbourg, guests have easy access to both the town's vibrant offerings and the natural beauty of the surrounding region. Whether it's a stroll through the historic streets of Cherbourg or an excursion to the nearby coastal landscapes, La Couronne serves as a convenient and luxurious base for exploration.

As a reflection of its commitment to sustainability and community engagement, La Couronne actively participates in local initiatives. From supporting local farmers and artisans to implementing eco-friendly practices within the establishment, the hotel is dedicated to being a responsible and contributing member of the community.

In conclusion, La Couronne – Hotel Restaurant is not merely a place to stay and dine; it is an immersive experience that captures the heart and soul of Normandy. With its historic charm, luxurious accommodations, and Michelin-starred dining, La Couronne stands as a testament to the timeless allure of French hospitality. Whether you are a discerning traveler in search of a unique retreat or a gastronome eager to explore the culinary treasures of Normandy, La Couronne invites you to indulge in an experience that transcends the ordinary.

CHAPTER 6: PRACTICAL INFORMATION

Normandy Currency and Banking

Normandy, situated in the northern part of France, is not only renowned for its picturesque landscapes and historical significance but also for its vibrant economic activities. Understanding the currency and banking system is crucial for travelers exploring this charming region. This section delves into the currency used, banking infrastructure, and practical tips for managing finances during your visit to Normandy.

The official currency of France, and consequently Normandy, is the Euro (€). As a member of the European Union, France adopted the Euro as its official currency in 2002, replacing the French Franc. The Euro is denoted by the symbol € and is divided into 100 cents. This uniform currency simplifies transactions for travelers moving across European countries, eliminating the need for currency exchange at every border.

Banking services in Normandy are modern, efficient, and widely accessible. The region is equipped with a network of banks, ATMs, and financial institutions that cater to the diverse needs of residents and visitors alike. Major cities such as Rouen, Caen, and Le Havre host various banks, ranging from global entities to local establishments.

ATMs, known as "Distributeurs Automatiques de Billets" (DAB), are conveniently scattered across cities and towns in Normandy. These ATMs accept major credit and debit cards, including Visa, MasterCard, and Maestro. Withdrawing Euros from ATMs is a straightforward process, and machines typically offer instructions in multiple languages to assist international visitors.

Credit cards are widely accepted in hotels, restaurants, shops, and tourist attractions throughout Normandy. Major credit card brands such as Visa and MasterCard are commonly used, while American Express and other cards may be accepted in certain establishments. However, it's advisable to carry some cash, especially when venturing into rural areas where card acceptance may be limited.

Traveler's checks, once a popular form of currency for international travelers, have become less common due to the widespread use of credit and debit cards. While some banks may still honor traveler's checks, it's advisable to check in advance and be prepared with alternative payment methods.

Foreign currency exchange services are available at banks and currency exchange offices in larger cities. These services may have varying exchange rates and fees, so it's recommended to compare rates before making transactions. Additionally, some hotels and businesses may offer currency exchange, but the rates might not be as competitive as those provided by dedicated exchange services.

When managing finances in Normandy, it's essential to be aware of banking hours. Banks typically operate from Monday to Friday, with reduced hours on Saturdays, and are closed on Sundays and public holidays. ATMs, on the other hand, offer convenient access to cash outside of regular banking hours.

In terms of financial etiquette, tipping is customary in restaurants, cafes, and for certain services. While service charges are often included in the bill, leaving a small tip for excellent service is appreciated. When paying with a credit card, it's common to leave the tip in cash.

In conclusion, navigating the currency and banking landscape in Normandy is a seamless experience for travelers. The Euro serves as the primary currency, and with the prevalence of ATMs and card acceptance, managing finances becomes convenient. As you explore the rich history and breathtaking scenery of Normandy, understanding the local currency and banking practices ensures a smooth and enjoyable travel experience.

Normandy Language

Normandy, a region in northern France, is not only renowned for its picturesque landscapes and historical significance but also for its rich linguistic heritage. The language spoken in Normandy has undergone a fascinating evolution, shaped by centuries of cultural, political, and social influences. This linguistic tapestry reflects the region's complex history and its interactions with neighboring areas.

At its core, the linguistic identity of Normandy is deeply rooted in the broader context of the French language. The majority of the population speaks French, the official language of the country. However, what makes Normandy linguistically distinct is the presence of regional languages and dialects that have left an indelible mark on the local linguistic landscape.

One of the most notable linguistic elements in Normandy is the Norman language, also known as "Norman." This Romance language has its origins in the medieval Norse-speaking population that settled in the region during the Viking invasions. Over time, Norman evolved as a unique blend of Old Norse and Old French, creating a linguistic bridge between the two cultures.

Though less prevalent in modern times, traces of Norman persist in local expressions, idioms, and even family names.

Beyond Norman, several regional dialects and languages have contributed to the linguistic diversity of Normandy. In areas close to the border with Brittany, the Gallo language has historically been spoken. Gallo is a Romance language closely related to French but distinct enough to be recognized as a separate linguistic entity. Its influence is most evident in the vocabulary and pronunciation of communities along the Breton-Norman border.

In addition to the historical impact of Norse and Breton languages, the Anglo-Norman dialect played a crucial role in shaping the linguistic landscape of Normandy. Following the Norman Conquest of England in 1066, the Anglo-Norman dialect became the language of the English aristocracy and administration. This linguistic connection endured for several centuries, leaving a lasting imprint on both Norman and English vocabulary.

The linguistic diversity of Normandy also extends "o the maritime vocabulary influenced by the region's coastal character. Fishing communities along the Normandy coastline have developed specialized terminologies related to their seafaring activities. These terms, often unique to specific regions, highlight the close connection between the people of Normandy and the sea.

Despite the historical significance of these regional languages and dialects, the linguistic landscape of Normandy has witnessed a gradual shift towards standard French. Modernization, urbanization, and increased connectivity have contributed to the homogenization of language, with younger generations predominantly using French in both formal and informal settings.

In recent years, there has been a growing awareness and effort to preserve and promote the regional languages of Normandy. Cultural organizations, language enthusiasts, and educators have worked towards revitalizing languages like Norman and Gallo. Initiatives include language courses, cultural events, and publications aimed at fostering a renewed appreciation for the linguistic diversity that defines Normandy's identity.

In conclusion, the linguistic tapestry of Normandy is a fascinating reflection of its rich history and cultural interactions. From the Norse influences of the Viking era to the enduring legacy of the Anglo-Norman dialect, the region's languages and dialects tell a story of resilience, adaptation, and cultural exchange. While French remains the dominant language, the preservation efforts underway underscore the importance of embracing and celebrating the linguistic diversity that continues to shape Normandy's identity.

Normandy Local Etiquette

Normandy, a region steeped in history and tradition, boasts a unique set of local etiquettes that reflect the warmth and authenticity of its people. As a traveler venturing into the picturesque landscapes and charming villages of Normandy, understanding and respecting these cultural nuances will undoubtedly enhance your overall experience.

In Normandy, greetings hold a special significance. A firm handshake accompanied by direct eye contact is the norm, signaling sincerity and respect. While the French tend to be more formal in their greetings, Normans infuse a genuine warmth into their interactions, making visitors feel welcome and appreciated.

The importance of mealtime etiquette cannot be overstated in Normandy. Sharing a meal is a cherished social activity, and punctuality is key. If invited to someone's home, it is customary to bring a small gift, such as flowers or a bottle of local cider. During the meal, maintain a polite pace and savor each course, as meals are not just about nourishment but are opportunities for bonding and camaraderie.

Politeness extends beyond the dining table to everyday encounters. It is customary to say "Bonjour" when entering a shop or any public space, a simple yet meaningful gesture that reflects courtesy. Learning a few basic French phrases will not only be appreciated but will also go a long way in breaking down language barriers and fostering connections with the locals.

In the rural landscapes of Normandy, where agriculture plays a significant role, a wave or a nod of acknowledgment to passing strangers is customary, creating a sense of community even among those who may be miles apart. This simple act encapsulates the friendliness that characterizes Norman villages.

Religious and historical sites are scattered throughout Normandy, and when visiting these places, it is essential to observe a respectful demeanor. Silence is often expected, especially in churches, where locals come to reflect and pray. Modest attire is also appreciated as a sign of reverence.

Normandy's festivals and events offer a unique insight into local customs. Whether it's the lively celebrations of Bastille Day or the solemn commemorations of D-Day, participating in these events provides a glimpse into the region's rich heritage. Attending with an open mind and a willingness to embrace the local customs will undoubtedly endear you to the people of Normandy.

In the bustling markets of Normandy, bargaining is not a common practice. Prices are generally fixed, and attempting to haggle may be perceived as impolite. Instead, engage in friendly

conversation with the vendors, showing genuine interest in their products. This approach is more likely to result in a positive and enriching interaction.

Normans take pride in their regional specialties, particularly their world-renowned cheeses and apple-based products. When sampling these delicacies, express your appreciation, as it is a gesture that transcends language and communicates a genuine enjoyment of the local culture.

As with any destination, respecting the environment is crucial in Normandy. Whether exploring the rugged coastline or strolling through apple orchards, adhere to designated paths and exercise responsible tourism. This preserves the natural beauty of the region and ensures that future generations can continue to enjoy its splendors.

In conclusion, immersing oneself in the local etiquette of Normandy is not just a matter of observing customs; it is a gateway to authentic experiences and meaningful connections. By embracing the warmth, courtesy, and traditions of this enchanting region, travelers can forge lasting memories and leave with a profound appreciation for the charm that defines Normandy.

Made in the USA
Monee, IL
02 June 2024

59264354R00075